MATH

Grade 5

Thomas J. Richards
Mathematics Teacher
Lamar Junior-Senior High School
Lamar, Missouri

 **McGraw-Hill**
Children's Publishing

Columbus, Ohio

Photo Credits

G. A. Heaviside/Photo Edit, 134; Cameron Mitchell, 2, 46, 114;
Alan Oddie/Photo Edit, 134; USDA Photo, 32

McGraw-Hill
Children's Publishing

A Division of The **McGraw·Hill** Companies

Send all inquiries to:
McGraw-Hill Children's Publishing
8787 Orion Place
Columbus, Ohio 43240-4027

ISBN 1-56189-905-4

1 2 3 4 5 6 7 8 9 10 VHG 06 05 04 03 02

Table of Contents

The SPECTRUM

Contents

MATHEMATICS Series
of Units

Using This Book

SPECTRUM MATHEMATICS is a non-graded, consumable series for students who need special help with the basic skills of computation and problem solving. This successful series emphasizes skill development and practice, without complex terminology or abstract symbolism. Because of the nature of the content and the students for whom the series is intended, readability has been carefully controlled to comply with the mathematics level of each book.

Features:

• A **Pre-Test** at the beginning of each chapter helps determine a student's understanding of the chapter content. The Pre-Test enables students and teachers to identify specific skills that need attention.

• **Developmental exercises** are provided at the top of the page when new skills are introduced. These exercises involve students in learning and serve as an aid for individualized instruction or independent study.

• **Abundant opportunities for practice** follow the developmental exercises.

• **Problem-solving pages** enable students to apply skills to realistic problems they will meet in everyday life.

• A **Test** at the end of each chapter gives students and teachers an opportunity to check understanding. A **Mid-Book Test**, covering Chapters 1–7, and a **Final Test**, covering all chapters, provide for further checks of understanding.

• A **Record of Test Scores** is provided on page xvi of this book so students can chart their progress as they complete each chapter test.

• **Answers** to all problems and test items are included at the back of the book.

This is the third edition of *SPECTRUM MATHEMATICS*. The basic books have remained the same. Some new, useful features have been added.

New Features:

• **Scope and Sequence Charts** for the entire Spectrum Mathematics series are included on pages iv–v.

• **Basic Facts Tests** for addition, subtraction, multiplication, and division are included on pages vii–xiv. There are two forms of each test. These may be given at any time the student or teacher decides they are appropriate.

• An **Assignment Record Sheet** is provided on page xv.

Addition Facts (Form A)

	a	*b*	*c*	*d*	*e*	*f*	*g*	*h*
1.	2 +2	5 +3	1 +1	8 +4	7 +1	0 +4	6 +3	3 +2
2.	7 +2	4 +1	6 +4	8 +0	4 +8	3 +7	4 +9	9 +3
3.	6 +5	0 +0	3 +8	8 +3	9 +5	6 +2	9 +0	2 +9
4.	4 +2	1 +3	5 +2	0 +2	9 +4	3 +6	8 +2	4 +7
5.	5 +4	8 +5	6 +6	2 +3	7 +3	2 +1	0 +7	1 +4
6.	9 +6	4 +3	7 +4	3 +5	5 +1	5 +5	8 +9	8 +1
7.	2 +4	9 +2	5 +9	9 +9	6 +7	2 +8	7 +5	4 +6
8.	8 +6	3 +4	2 +5	5 +6	7 +0	7 +6	9 +8	2 +7
9.	7 +9	4 +4	9 +1	6 +8	7 +8	5 +7	3 +9	8 +8
10.	6 +9	9 +7	3 +3	5 +8	2 +6	8 +7	4 +5	7 +7

Perfect score: 80   My score: _____

Addition Facts (Form B)

	a	*b*	*c*	*d*	*e*	*f*	*g*	*h*
1.	5 +2	1 +3	6 +6	0 +5	4 +0	3 +2	8 +3	2 +4
2.	3 +3	7 +1	2 +1	5 +8	7 +9	4 +4	6 +0	3 +6
3.	4 +3	0 +8	9 +2	7 +8	9 +9	0 +3	6 +7	4 +9
4.	5 +7	8 +4	3 +7	4 +8	6 +2	2 +2	5 +9	1 +1
5.	8 +9	1 +5	0 +0	4 +2	6 +8	8 +5	6 +5	4 +7
6.	2 +5	9 +7	5 +6	8 +2	3 +5	2 +8	9 +3	7 +2
7.	1 +6	6 +3	3 +8	9 +5	5 +5	7 +7	4 +5	2 +9
8.	6 +9	4 +6	8 +7	2 +6	1 +8	9 +8	7 +3	5 +4
9.	7 +5	8 +0	3 +4	7 +4	9 +6	4 +1	0 +9	8 +6
10.	2 +7	8 +8	5 +3	9 +4	3 +9	6 +4	7 +6	1 +9

Perfect score: 80   My score: _____

Subtraction Facts (Form A)

	a	b	c	d	e	f	g	h
1.	6 −5	1 4 −6	7 −2	1 1 −8	9 −4	1 0 −7	7 −6	1 4 −9
2.	9 −7	1 2 −5	7 −5	1 7 −8	8 −8	1 1 −4	6 −3	1 2 −8
3.	6 −6	1 0 −8	9 −2	1 1 −5	6 −2	1 5 −9	8 −6	1 3 −6
4.	1 1 −2	1 6 −7	7 −3	1 2 −9	5 −5	1 1 −7	8 −3	1 2 −4
5.	1 0 −1	1 5 −6	8 −7	1 0 −6	7 −1	1 0 −3	5 −2	1 3 −9
6.	9 −6	1 7 −9	2 −1	1 2 −3	8 −4	1 0 −5	9 −8	1 6 −8
7.	7 −7	1 5 −8	4 −2	1 6 −9	1 −1	1 3 −5	3 −1	1 0 −9
8.	9 −5	1 3 −4	8 −0	1 5 −7	9 −1	1 2 −6	7 −0	1 3 −8
9.	1 1 −3	1 2 −7	8 −1	1 1 −6	9 −0	1 1 −9	8 −5	1 4 −7
10.	1 8 −9	1 0 −4	9 −9	1 3 −7	1 0 −2	1 4 −8	9 −3	1 4 −5

Perfect score: 80   My score: _____

ix

Subtraction Facts (Form B)

	a	*b*	*c*	*d*	*e*	*f*	*g*	*h*
1.	10 −6	9 −1	11 −3	8 −2	12 −3	5 −0	10 −1	9 −5
2.	11 −7	4 −0	12 −5	10 −9	11 −4	9 −8	13 −4	8 −8
3.	12 −6	9 −7	10 −2	5 −5	12 −8	9 −3	11 −6	6 −0
4.	14 −5	11 −9	12 −4	9 −6	11 −5	8 −1	13 −7	7 −3
5.	12 −7	18 −9	13 −6	6 −6	14 −7	7 −0	11 −2	8 −6
6.	10 −3	9 −2	10 −5	5 −1	13 −8	6 −5	17 −8	7 −1
7.	11 −8	8 −3	12 −9	8 −0	16 −8	8 −7	10 −4	13 −9
8.	10 −7	7 −5	15 −8	6 −2	14 −6	14 −9	15 −7	9 −4
9.	17 −9	6 −1	9 −9	8 −4	15 −9	7 −2	14 −8	8 −5
10.	13 −5	9 −0	16 −9	7 −6	16 −7	10 −8	15 −6	7 −7

Perfect score: 80   My score: _____

Multiplication Facts (Form A)

	a	b	c	d	e	f	g	h
1.	9 ×1	4 ×2	3 ×7	1 ×4	9 ×3	5 ×9	8 ×8	2 ×6
2.	4 ×9	7 ×7	2 ×0	6 ×5	3 ×6	1 ×2	7 ×6	6 ×4
3.	3 ×4	0 ×0	6 ×6	7 ×5	4 ×8	8 ×7	5 ×3	4 ×0
4.	6 ×0	8 ×9	3 ×8	8 ×0	1 ×8	7 ×8	4 ×7	8 ×6
5.	2 ×5	5 ×4	7 ×4	0 ×3	9 ×4	2 ×2	9 ×9	1 ×1
6.	8 ×1	1 ×5	6 ×7	7 ×9	3 ×1	8 ×5	3 ×5	6 ×3
7.	4 ×3	6 ×1	5 ×5	6 ×8	4 ×6	9 ×8	1 ×0	7 ×1
8.	6 ×9	0 ×5	8 ×4	3 ×3	7 ×0	2 ×8	9 ×7	3 ×9
9.	5 ×6	9 ×5	1 ×9	5 ×2	5 ×7	9 ×2	4 ×5	7 ×2
10.	3 ×2	6 ×2	8 ×3	4 ×4	0 ×9	7 ×3	5 ×8	9 ×6

Perfect score: 80   My score: _____

Multiplication Facts (Form B)

	a	*b*	*c*	*d*	*e*	*f*	*g*	*h*
1.	5 ×5	4 ×3	1 ×1	7 ×3	6 ×2	0 ×7	8 ×1	3 ×4
2.	6 ×3	9 ×7	2 ×1	3 ×3	8 ×2	4 ×1	9 ×5	2 ×8
3.	2 ×9	0 ×8	5 ×6	1 ×3	5 ×2	2 ×2	0 ×0	9 ×3
4.	3 ×5	4 ×4	8 ×3	7 ×2	0 ×1	4 ×9	8 ×8	3 ×0
5.	9 ×2	6 ×4	0 ×2	9 ×4	6 ×5	3 ×8	2 ×3	5 ×0
6.	5 ×1	7 ×4	8 ×4	2 ×4	9 ×6	5 ×7	7 ×9	8 ×7
7.	9 ×1	1 ×7	7 ×5	0 ×4	4 ×5	9 ×9	5 ×8	4 ×8
8.	6 ×8	8 ×5	5 ×9	6 ×6	7 ×7	0 ×6	5 ×3	3 ×9
9.	2 ×5	3 ×6	9 ×8	1 ×6	8 ×6	4 ×7	7 ×8	6 ×9
10.	5 ×4	7 ×6	8 ×9	4 ×6	9 ×0	6 ×7	3 ×7	2 ×7

Perfect score: 80   My score: _____

Division Facts (Form A)

	a	*b*	*c*	*d*	*e*	*f*	*g*
1.	2⟌6	9⟌18	3⟌15	6⟌18	1⟌3	4⟌12	5⟌45
2.	5⟌35	4⟌8	7⟌0	1⟌7	4⟌36	9⟌27	8⟌16
3.	2⟌8	6⟌24	9⟌36	3⟌18	4⟌16	7⟌7	3⟌12
4.	8⟌0	9⟌9	2⟌10	5⟌40	2⟌4	8⟌24	6⟌54
5.	2⟌2	6⟌0	4⟌32	3⟌21	9⟌45	3⟌9	7⟌14
6.	7⟌63	1⟌9	9⟌0	8⟌32	6⟌48	5⟌0	2⟌14
7.	5⟌30	4⟌28	7⟌56	2⟌12	8⟌72	1⟌5	9⟌54
8.	3⟌0	6⟌42	3⟌24	7⟌21	4⟌4	6⟌12	2⟌0
9.	7⟌28	8⟌40	5⟌25	7⟌49	5⟌5	9⟌63	8⟌64
10.	4⟌20	6⟌6	4⟌0	6⟌36	2⟌16	5⟌10	3⟌3
11.	1⟌8	5⟌20	4⟌24	9⟌72	8⟌56	7⟌42	3⟌27
12.	8⟌48	9⟌81	7⟌35	3⟌6	5⟌15	2⟌18	6⟌30

Perfect score: 84   My score: _____

Division Facts (Form B)

	a	b	c	d	e	f	g
1.	$3\overline{)18}$	$5\overline{)35}$	$4\overline{)4}$	$1\overline{)9}$	$7\overline{)0}$	$2\overline{)18}$	$4\overline{)36}$
2.	$6\overline{)54}$	$7\overline{)14}$	$2\overline{)16}$	$5\overline{)40}$	$4\overline{)8}$	$6\overline{)42}$	$7\overline{)63}$
3.	$1\overline{)0}$	$8\overline{)24}$	$4\overline{)32}$	$7\overline{)21}$	$1\overline{)6}$	$5\overline{)45}$	$3\overline{)0}$
4.	$5\overline{)30}$	$2\overline{)14}$	$6\overline{)48}$	$3\overline{)21}$	$7\overline{)28}$	$8\overline{)16}$	$9\overline{)9}$
5.	$3\overline{)15}$	$9\overline{)0}$	$1\overline{)5}$	$9\overline{)18}$	$3\overline{)6}$	$6\overline{)12}$	$8\overline{)40}$
6.	$7\overline{)35}$	$1\overline{)4}$	$8\overline{)48}$	$4\overline{)12}$	$8\overline{)8}$	$3\overline{)24}$	$5\overline{)0}$
7.	$2\overline{)12}$	$9\overline{)45}$	$4\overline{)0}$	$4\overline{)28}$	$1\overline{)3}$	$9\overline{)27}$	$6\overline{)36}$
8.	$4\overline{)24}$	$5\overline{)25}$	$2\overline{)10}$	$9\overline{)72}$	$5\overline{)10}$	$1\overline{)2}$	$8\overline{)56}$
9.	$6\overline{)24}$	$8\overline{)0}$	$7\overline{)49}$	$3\overline{)9}$	$4\overline{)20}$	$7\overline{)56}$	$2\overline{)0}$
10.	$3\overline{)12}$	$9\overline{)81}$	$1\overline{)1}$	$6\overline{)18}$	$5\overline{)15}$	$2\overline{)4}$	$9\overline{)54}$
11.	$6\overline{)6}$	$5\overline{)20}$	$6\overline{)30}$	$9\overline{)36}$	$2\overline{)8}$	$8\overline{)64}$	$3\overline{)27}$
12.	$8\overline{)32}$	$2\overline{)6}$	$8\overline{)72}$	$4\overline{)16}$	$6\overline{)0}$	$9\overline{)63}$	$7\overline{)42}$

Perfect score: 84   My score: _____

Assignment Record Sheet

NAME _____

Pages Assigned	Date	Score

Pages Assigned	Date	Score

Pages Assigned	Date	Score

SPECTRUM MATHEMATICS

Record of Test Scores

Rank	Test Pages													
	13	25	35	47	57	69	77	87	101	119	135	142	143–4	145–8
Excellent	25	20	20	20	20	20	20	20	18	20	20	20	40	100
Very Good	20	15	15	15	15	15	15	15	15	15	15	15	30	80
Good	15	10	10	10	10	10	10	10	10	10	10	10	20	60
Fair	10													40
Poor	5	5	5	5	5	5	5	5	5	5	5	5	10	20
	0	0	0	0	0	0	0	0	0	0	0	0	0	0

To record the score you receive on a TEST:

(1) Find the vertical scale below the page number of that TEST,

(2) on that vertical scale, draw a ● at the mark which represents your score.

For example, if your score for the TEST on page 13 is "My score: 15," draw a ● at the 15-mark on the first vertical scale. A score of 15 would show that your rank is "Good." You can check your progress from one test to the next by connecting the dots with a line segment.

PRE-TEST—Addition and Subtraction

Add or subtract.

	a	b	c	d	e
1.	42 +26	37 +48	23 +95	76 +48	48 +39
2.	84 −23	75 −26	173 −92	165 −87	108 −39
3.	421 +357	832 +149	267 +138	521 +783	956 +287
4.	854 −321	783 −625	921 −570	1436 −349	1793 −875
5.	4235 +3796	6518 +4739	51672 +4318	52196 +38417	25186 +35821
6.	7659 −3847	8250 −6374	52169 −3057	42196 −38427	52105 −38156
7.	42 57 +38	34 27 +86	375 246 +381	6023 4034 +7012	73152 43081 +52165
8.	54 27 38 +46	731 208 319 +426	500 364 217 390 +324	8216 4315 2173 4081 +5216	70812 32181 31218 61408 +30802

Perfect score: 40   My score: _____

Problem Solving Pre-Test

Kennedy 33   Clark 24
Time   3:01
QTR   3

Solve each problem.

1. How many points have been scored by both teams?

Kennedy has scored _____ points.

Clark has scored _____ points.

Both teams have scored _____ points.

2. Which team is ahead? By how many points are they ahead?

_____ is ahead.

They are ahead by _____ points.

3. During the rest of the game Kennedy scored 10 more points and Clark scored 12 more points. Which team won the game? By how many points did they win?

The final score for Kennedy was _____.

The final score for Clark was _____.

_____ won the game.

They won by _____ points.

1.

2.

3.

Perfect score: 9   My score: _____

Lesson 1   Addition

Add.

	a	*b*	*c*	*d*	*e*	*f*	*g*	*h*
1.	3 +6	7 +4	4 +3	5 +9	6 +1	6 +8	3 +7	9 +2
2.	8 +3	9 +5	8 +8	0 +5	6 +7	8 +2	7 +1	5 +7
3.	7 +9	4 +8	7 +2	3 +3	6 +6	4 +7	9 +1	6 +3
4.	6 +4	6 +9	2 +8	7 +7	8 +9	4 +2	4 +1	6 +2
5.	6 +5	4 +6	4 +4	3 +8	5 +2	7 +6	8 +0	3 +9
6.	5 +8	8 +1	3 +2	9 +3	7 +8	8 +6	7 +3	9 +8
7.	2 +7	9 +0	9 +6	2 +2	5 +4	8 +7	1 +9	7 +0
8.	3 +5	9 +7	5 +5	4 +9	9 +4	0 +7	3 +4	5 +6
9.	2 +5	8 +4	9 +9	7 +5	5 +3	2 +9	8 +5	2 +6

Perfect score: 72   My score: _____

Lesson 2 Subtraction

Subtract.

	a	b	c	d	e	f	g	h
1.	7 −2	1 1 −5	8 −4	1 3 −8	7 −0	8 −1	1 4 −8	1 7 −9
2.	8 −3	1 1 −4	9 −2	1 4 −9	1 2 −8	1 1 −7	4 −0	1 0 −1
3.	1 1 −3	9 −5	1 3 −6	1 2 −9	1 0 −8	1 0 −2	1 1 −6	1 5 −9
4.	1 5 −8	1 1 −2	1 0 −3	1 6 −9	1 4 −7	1 4 −5	1 2 −4	7 −3
5.	8 −2	1 3 −9	1 6 −8	1 8 −9	6 −0	9 −8	6 −4	1 3 −5
6.	8 −7	1 5 −7	1 0 −4	7 −5	1 2 −6	1 3 −4	1 3 −7	6 −2
7.	9 −4	1 0 −9	1 0 −7	9 −1	1 2 −3	8 −0	1 0 −6	1 6 −7
8.	1 4 −6	1 0 −5	1 1 −9	6 −5	5 −2	9 −7	1 5 −6	9 −6
9.	1 2 −7	8 −6	9 −3	1 7 −8	1 1 −8	8 −5	1 2 −5	7 −4

Perfect score: 72   My score: _____

4

Lesson 3   Addition and Subtraction

	Add the ones. Rename.	Add the tens.		Rename 146 as "1 hundred, 3 tens, and 16 ones." Then subtract the ones.	Rename 1 hundred and 3 tens as "13 tens." Then subtract the tens.

58 +89	8 +9 1 7	58 +89 7	58 +89 147	146 −87	1 4 6 − 8 7 9	1 4 6 − 8 7 5 9

Add.

	a	b	c	d	e	f
1.	23 +54	63 +25	72 +16	43 +54	26 +31	27 +42
2.	27 +35	47 +28	65 +26	31 +49	56 +28	39 +26
3.	47 +78	57 +86	32 +79	67 +84	36 +96	56 +47
4.	36 +27	45 +23	77 +77	63 +42	56 +24	35 +75

Subtract.

5.	76 −24	37 −22	89 −63	75 −24	65 −31	49 −30
6.	95 −26	38 −19	52 −27	65 −48	91 −73	54 −27
7.	126 −37	143 −95	156 −88	172 −76	168 −99	153 −85

Perfect score: 42   My score: _____

Problem Solving

Solve each problem.

1. Sarah's father worked 36 hours one week and 47 hours the next week. How many hours did he work during these two weeks?

He worked _____ hours the first week.

He worked _____ hours the second week.

During these two weeks,
   he worked a total of _____ hours.

2. Seventy-six people live in Harold's apartment building. In Mike's apartment building, there are 85 people. How many more people live in Mike's building than in Harold's building?

_____ people live in Mike's building.

_____ people live in Harold's building.

_____ more people live in Mike's building.

3. In problem 2, how many people live in both Harold's and Mike's apartment buildings?

_____ people live in both buildings.

4. There are 103 pages in Vera's new book. She has read 35 pages. How many pages does she have left to read?

There are _____ pages in the book.

She has read _____ pages.

She has _____ pages left to read.

5. Paula lives 53 kilometers from Darton. Ann lives 85 kilometers from Darton. How many kilometers closer to Darton does Paula live than Ann?

Paula lives _____ kilometers closer.

1.

2.

3.

4.

5.

Perfect score: 11   My score: _____

6

Lesson 4   Addition and Subtraction

Add from right to left.

^{1} 754 +587	$^{1\ 1}$ 754 +587	$^{1\ 1}$ 754 +587
1	41	1341

Subtract from right to left.

$^{3\ 11}$ 1341 −587	^{13} $^{2\ 3\ 11}$ 1341 −587	$^{12\ 13}$ $^{2\ 3\ 11}$ 1341 −587
4	54	754

Add.

	a	b	c	d	e	f
1.	314 +482	703 +192	542 +318	265 +429	553 +274	629 +280
2.	483 +702	546 +931	736 +279	653 +199	706 +539	582 +609
3.	813 +792	763 +762	423 +798	358 +759	816 +395	926 +178

Subtract.

	a	b	c	d	e	f
4.	784 −362	927 −405	542 −314	765 −238	926 −341	563 −281
5.	1732 −812	1574 −923	1764 −925	1345 −629	1542 −286	1637 −439
6.	1563 −678	1322 −733	1580 −687	1629 −243	1435 −162	1748 −358
7.	1984 −362	1864 −372	1250 −741	1608 −413	1500 −263	1542 −245

Perfect score: 42   My score: _____

7

Problem Solving

Answer each question.

1. The mileage reading on Mr. Lee's car is 142. On Mr. Cook's, it is 319. How many more miles does Mr. Cook have on his car than Mr. Lee?

Are you to add
or subtract? _____

How many more miles does
Mr. Cook have on his car than Mr. Lee? _____

2. Myrtle and Doris collect trading stamps. Myrtle has 423 trading stamps and Doris has 519. How many stamps do both girls have?

Are you to add
or subtract? _____

How many stamps
do both girls have? _____

3. Helen's family drove 975 miles on their vacation last year and 776 miles this year. How many miles did they travel during these two vacations?

Are you to add
or subtract? _____

How many miles did they travel
during these two vacations? _____

4. In problem 3, how many more miles did they travel during the first year than the last?

Are you to add
or subtract? _____

How many more miles did they
travel during the first year than the last? _____

5. Tricia needs 293 more points to win a prize. It takes 1,500 points to win a prize. How many points does Tricia have now?

Are you to add
or subtract? _____

How many points does she have now? _____

1.
2.
3.
4.
5.

Perfect score: 10   My score: _____

8

Lesson 5   Addition and Subtraction

Add.
21345
+9462
30807

Check. { −9462
21345

These should
be the same.

Subtract.
30807
−9462
21345

Check. { +9462
30807

These should
be the same.

Add. Check each answer.

	a	b	c
1.	30821 +4163	52964 +3175	76487 +5243
2.	42563 +15786	15243 +27561	36724 +81409

Subtract. Check each answer.

3.	72431 −5316	92640 −6741	61430 −6429
4.	54061 −6835	72413 −6785	84205 −5116

Perfect score: 12   My score: _____

9

Problem Solving

Solve each problem. Check each answer.

1. The space flight is expected to last 11,720 minutes. They are now 7,342 minutes into the flight. How many minutes remain?

_____ minutes remain in the flight.

2. In one year Mr. Ching drove the company car 13,428 kilometers and his personal car 8,489 kilometers. How many kilometers did he drive both cars?

He drove _____ kilometers.

3. In problem 2, how many fewer kilometers did he drive his personal car than the company car?

He drove his personal car _____ fewer kilometers.

4. The factory where Mrs. Whitmal works produced 3,173 fewer parts this month than last. The factory produced 42,916 parts this month. How many parts did it produce last month?

The factory produced _____ parts last month.

5. Suppose the factory in problem 4 produced 3,173 more parts this month than last. How many parts would it have produced last month?

_____ parts would have been produced.

6. There are 86,400 seconds in a day. How many seconds are there in two days?

There are _____ seconds in two days.

7. During one month Jo Anne spends 14,400 minutes sleeping and 5,800 minutes eating. How much time does she spend either eating or sleeping?

She spends _____ minutes either eating or sleeping.

| 1. |
| 2. |
| 3. |
| 4. |
| 5. |
| 6. |
| 7. |

Perfect score: 7   My score: _____

10

Lesson 6 Addition

Add the ones.

3675	5 3675	
1406	6 1406	
3759	9 3759	
+6134	+4 +6134	
	(2)4 4	

$$\begin{array}{r} 3675 \\ 1406 \\ 3759 \\ +6134 \\ \hline 4 \end{array}$$

Follow the same pattern to add the tens, the hundreds, and so on.

$$\begin{array}{r} {\scriptstyle 1\ 1\ 2} \\ 3675 \\ 1406 \\ 3759 \\ +6134 \\ \hline 14974 \end{array}$$

Add.

	a	*b*	*c*	*d*	*e*
1.	453 216 +320	231 425 +317	242 375 +161	726 630 +712	542 416 +537
2.	6314 2145 +7634	2165 3420 +7015	8093 1246 +543	72193 83470 +21659	72165 45230 +3216
3.	325 463 179 +258	726 314 540 +829	7316 1425 7834 +2401	8216 7343 81692 +40830	92163 48517 73214 +82119
4.	730 460 273 892 +453	3829 1364 1274 429 +670	8213 4106 2300 4819 +2745	36000 72450 83192 62451 +31924	42165 30708 29115 40082 +31621
5.	542 365 421 300 460 +523	1628 329 1754 321 608 +2911	4216 53008 42134 2165 3008 +4000	52163 4218 316 5421 62190 +420	316 2143 126 52140 1230 +680

Perfect score: 25   My score: _____

11

Problem Solving

Solve each problem.

1. During the summer reading program, Faye read 752 pages. Barbara read 436 pages. Gilbert read 521 pages. How many pages did these students read altogether?

They read _____ pages altogether.

2. During September Joe Shedare traveled the following numbers of miles: 421; 308; 240; and 571. What was the total number of miles he traveled?

He traveled a total of _____ miles.

3. Four astronauts have logged the following times in actual space travel: 4,216 minutes, 14,628 minutes, 3,153 minutes, and 22,117 minutes. How many minutes have all four astronauts logged in actual space travel?

All four have logged _____ minutes in space.

4. The number of parts shipped to 6 cities was as follows: 317; 2,410; 32,415; 4,068; 321; and 5,218. How many parts were shipped in all?

_____ parts were shipped.

5. A recent census gave the following populations: Adel, 4,321; Albany, 55,890; Alma, 3,515; Alto Park, 2,526; Americus, 13,472; and Ashburn, 3,291. What is the total population of these places?

The total population is _____.

6. In an earlier census, the populations of the towns listed in problem 5 were 2,776; 31,155; 2,588; 1,195; 11,389; and 2,918 respectively. What was the total population then?

Then the total population was _____.

7. In problem 5, what is the total population of Adel, Albany, and Alto Park?

The total population is _____.

| 1 |
| 2. |
| 3. |
| 4. |
| 5. |
| 6. |
| 7. |

Perfect score: 7   My score: _____

CHAPTER 1 TEST

Add or subtract.

	a	b	c	d	e
1.	46 +32	423 +268	1829 +3573	7521 +3609	52163 +72845
2.	85 −32	564 −382	1936 −479	18312 −9264	10306 −2568
3.	32 26 +13	724 380 +465	295 327 168 +269	5534 1468 3137 +2950	42163 30820 21911 +60422
4.	7832 −1467	8309 −2654	13182 −4296	171234 −82169	102085 −36526

Solve each problem.

5. The following points were earned in a ticket-selling contest: Maxine, 2,320; Trudy, 1,564; Eileen, 907; Lyn, 852; Marty, 775. What was the total number of points earned by Maxine and Eileen?

Maxine earned _____ points.

Eileen earned _____ points.

They earned a total of _____ points.

6. In problem 5, what was the total number of points earned by all five girls?

They earned a total of _____ points.

7. In problem 5, how many more points did Trudy earn than Marty?

Trudy earned _____ more points.

5.

6.　　　　**7.**

Perfect score: 25　　My score: _____

PRE-TEST—Multiplication

Multiply.

	a	b	c	d
1.	24 ×2	35 ×2	154 ×6	678 ×9
2.	31 ×23	82 ×18	45 ×51	87 ×39
3.	143 ×22	734 ×19	253 ×62	708 ×36
4.	321 ×123	432 ×621	507 ×143	821 ×105
5.	3126 ×422	4032 ×145	3124 ×712	8197 ×325

Perfect score: 20   My score: _____

Lesson 1 Multiplication

Multiply.

	a	b	c	d	e	f	g	h
1.	4 ×2	8 ×2	7 ×2	2 ×2	6 ×2	5 ×2	3 ×2	1 ×2
2.	8 ×3	2 ×3	9 ×3	6 ×3	5 ×3	0 ×3	4 ×3	3 ×3
3.	2 ×4	1 ×4	6 ×4	8 ×4	7 ×4	3 ×4	9 ×4	4 ×4
4.	7 ×5	5 ×5	2 ×5	6 ×5	4 ×5	9 ×5	3 ×5	8 ×5
5.	6 ×6	2 ×6	9 ×6	3 ×6	1 ×6	7 ×6	5 ×6	8 ×6
6.	1 ×7	3 ×7	9 ×7	2 ×7	6 ×7	7 ×7	8 ×7	5 ×7
7.	5 ×8	1 ×8	7 ×8	2 ×8	9 ×8	6 ×8	3 ×8	8 ×8
8.	8 ×9	2 ×9	1 ×9	6 ×9	7 ×9	4 ×9	5 ×9	9 ×9
9.	3 ×0	8 ×0	0 ×0	1 ×0	6 ×1	2 ×1	9 ×1	7 ×1

Perfect score: 72   My score: _____

Problem Solving

Solve each problem.

1. There are 6 rows of desks in the office. Each row has 8 desks. How many desks are in the office?

There are _____ rows of desks.

There are _____

There are _____

2. There are 9 row___
row. How many tree___

There are _____

There are _____

There are _____

3. The people at the p___
people each. Nine teams ___ ___ ___ many people
were in the park?

Each team has _____ people.

There were _____ teams formed.

There were _____ people in the park.

4. There were 6 people in each car. There were 7 cars. How many people were there in all?

There were _____ people in each car.

There were _____ cars.

There were _____ people in all.

5. How many cents would you need to buy eight 8-cent pencils?

You would need _____ cents.

6. There are 5 oranges in each sack. How many oranges would there be in 9 sacks?

There would be _____ oranges in 9 sacks.

1.

4.

5.	6.

Perfect score: 14   My score: _____

16

Lesson 2 Multiplication

Multiply
3 ones by 5.

Multiply 7 tens by 5.
Add the tens.

$$\begin{array}{r} 3 \\ \times 5 \\ \hline (1)\,5 \end{array}\qquad \begin{array}{r} 7\overset{1}{3} \\ \times 5 \\ \hline 5 \end{array}$$

$$\begin{array}{r} 7 \text{ tens} \\ \times 5 \\ \hline 35 \text{ tens} \\ +1 \text{ ten} \\ \hline 36 \text{ tens} \end{array}\qquad \begin{array}{r} \overset{1}{7}3 \\ \times 5 \\ \hline 365 \end{array}$$

$$\begin{array}{r} 32\overset{2}{7} \\ \times 4 \\ \hline 8 \end{array}\qquad \begin{array}{r} 3\overset{12}{2}7 \\ \times 4 \\ \hline 08 \end{array}\qquad \begin{array}{r} \overset{12}{3}27 \\ \times 4 \\ \hline 1308 \end{array}$$

Multiply.

	a	b	c	d	e	f
1.	32 ×2	21 ×3	42 ×2	132 ×2	213 ×3	421 ×2
2.	16 ×4	36 ×2	28 ×3	123 ×4	127 ×3	215 ×4
3.	73 ×3	42 ×4	81 ×5	352 ×2	172 ×4	263 ×3
4.	57 ×5	28 ×6	37 ×4	256 ×3	385 ×2	177 ×5
5.	28 ×6	47 ×8	39 ×5	426 ×7	358 ×6	234 ×5
6.	57 ×8	48 ×2	70 ×5	526 ×3	409 ×5	730 ×7
7.	72 ×9	95 ×7	81 ×8	629 ×8	801 ×7	658 ×9

Perfect score: 42   My score: _____

Problem Solving

Solve each problem.

1. Each club member works 3 hours each month. There are 32 members. What is the total number of hours worked each month by all the club members?

There are _____ club members.

Each member works _____ hours.

The club members work _____ hours in all.

2. Mrs. Robins drives 19 miles every working day. How many miles does she drive in a five-day work-week?

She drives _____ miles every working day.

She works _____ days a week.

She drives _____ miles in a five-day workweek.

3. It takes 54 minutes to make one gizmo. How long will it take to make 3 gizmos?

It takes _____ minutes to make one gizmo.

There are _____ gizmos.

It takes _____ minutes to make 3 gizmos.

4. Each box weighs 121 kilograms. There are 4 boxes. What is the total weight of the 4 boxes?

Each box weighs _____ kilograms.

There are _____ boxes.

The total weight of the 4 boxes is _____ kilograms.

5. There are 168 hours in a week. How many hours are there in 6 weeks?

There are _____ hours in 6 weeks.

6. There were 708 employees at work today. Each employee worked 8 hours. How many hours did these employees work?

_____ hours were worked.

1.

2.

3.

4.

5.

6.

Perfect score: 14   My score: _____

18

Lesson 3   Multiplication

```
  41        41        56        56
  ×2       ×20        ×3       ×30
 ___      ____      ____      _____
  82       820       168      1680
```

Multiply   Multiply
56 by 1.   56 by 30.

```
   56          56          56
  ×31         ×31         ×31
 ____        ____        ____
   56          56          56  ⎫
                         1680  ⎬ Add.
             1680              ⎭
                         _____
                          1736
```

If 2×41=82, then 20×41=_____.

If 3×56=168, then 30×56=_____.

If 4×27=108, then 40×27=_____.

Multiply.

	a	b	c	d	e	f
1.	23 ×3	23 ×30	43 ×2	43 ×20	51 ×4	51 ×40
2.	37 ×4	37 ×40	54 ×6	54 ×60	73 ×9	73 ×90
3.	42 ×30	75 ×20	54 ×40	62 ×70	84 ×60	32 ×50

Multiply.

	a	b	c	d	e
4.	31 ×23	42 ×33	45 ×12	17 ×35	36 ×24
5.	54 ×26	37 ×41	28 ×16	38 ×73	46 ×28

Perfect score: 28   My score: _____

19

Problem Solving

Solve each problem.

1. There are 60 minutes in one hour. How many minutes are there in 24 hours?

There are _____ minutes in 24 hours.

2. Forty-eight toy boats are packed in each box. How many boats are there in 16 boxes?

There are _____ boats in 16 boxes.

3. Seventy-three new cars can be assembled in one hour. At that rate, how many cars could be assembled in 51 hours?

_____ cars could be assembled in 51 hours.

4. A truck is hauling 36 bags of cement. Each bag weighs 94 pounds. How many pounds of cement are being hauled?

_____ pounds of cement are being hauled.

5. To square a number means to multiply the number by itself. What is the square of 68?

The square of 68 is _____.

6. Seventy-five books are packed in each box. How many books are there in 85 boxes?

There are _____ books in 85 boxes.

7. Every classroom in Jane's school has at least 29 desks. There are 38 classrooms in all. What is the least number of desks in the school?

There are at least _____ desks.

8. Some pupils came to the museum on 38 buses. There were 58 pupils on each bus. How many pupils came to the museum by bus?

_____ pupils came by bus.

1.	2.
3.	4.
5.	6.
7.	8.

Perfect score: 8   My score: _____

20

Lesson 4   Multiplication

Multiply   Multiply
351 by 7.   351 by 20.

```
  351        351         351         351
 ×27        ×27         ×27         ×27
           2457        2457        2457  ⎫
                       7020        7020  ⎬ Add.
                                   9477  ⎭
```

Multiply.

	a	b	c	d	e
1.	42 ×13	23 ×32	54 ×41	37 ×26	58 ×19
2.	58 ×72	27 ×36	40 ×55	27 ×27	39 ×42
3.	154 ×13	231 ×26	251 ×41	312 ×32	415 ×47
4.	365 ×27	426 ×13	715 ×26	302 ×43	756 ×29

Perfect score: 20   My score: _____

Problem Solving

Solve each problem.

1. A machine can produce 98 parts in one hour. How many parts could it produce in 72 hours?

It could produce _____ parts in 72 hours.

2. Each new bus can carry 66 passengers. How many passengers can ride on 85 new buses?

_____ passengers could ride on 85 buses.

3. A gross is twelve dozen or 144. The school ordered 21 gross of pencils. How many pencils were ordered?

The school ordered _____ pencils.

4. How many hours are there in a year (365 days)?

There are _____ hours in a year.

5. Each of 583 people worked a 40-hour week. How many hours of work was this?

It was _____ hours of work.

6. The highway mileage between New York and Chicago is 840 miles. How many miles would a bus travel in making 68 one-way trips between New York and Chicago?

The bus would travel _____ miles.

7. The airline distance between the cities in problem **6** is 713 miles. What is the least number of miles a plane would travel in making 57 one-way trips?

The least number of miles would be _____.

8. The rail mileage between Washington, D. C., and Chicago is 768 miles. How many miles would a train travel in making 52 one-way trips?

It would travel _____ miles.

9. The airline distance between the cities in problem **8** is 597 miles. What is the least number of miles a plane would travel in making 45 one-way trips?

The least number of miles would be _____.

1.	2.
3.	4.
5.	6.
7.	8.
9.	

Perfect score: 9   My score: _____

22

Lesson 5 Multiplication

3254	3254	3254		3254
×2	×20	×200		×213
6508	65080	650800		9762 ——— 3×3254
				32540 ——— 10×3254
				650800 ——— 200×3254
				693102 Add.

If 2×3254=6508, then 20×3254 = _____.

If 2×3254=6508, then 200×3254 = _____.

Multiply.

	a	*b*	*c*	*d*
1.	316 ×2	316 ×200	4281 ×3	4281 ×300
2.	416 ×213	375 ×291	408 ×316	219 ×503
3.	316 ×275	483 ×211	4231 ×213	3456 ×123
4.	2175 ×243	3216 ×208	3090 ×752	6613 ×342

Perfect score: 16   My score: _____

Problem Solving

Solve each problem.

1. Each crate the men unloaded weighed 342 pounds. They unloaded 212 crates. How many pounds did they unload?

The men unloaded _____ pounds.

2. The school cafeteria expects to serve 425 customers every day. At that rate, how many meals will be served if the cafeteria is open 175 days a year?

_____ meals will be served.

3. There are 168 hours in one week. How many hours are there in 260 weeks?

There are _____ hours in 260 weeks.

4. There are 3,600 seconds in one hour and 168 hours in one week. How many seconds are there in one week?

There are _____ seconds in one week.

5. A jet carrying 128 passengers flew 2,574 miles. How many passenger-miles (number of passengers times number of miles traveled) would this be?

It would be _____ passenger-miles.

6. How many passenger-miles would be flown by the jet in problem 5, if it flew from Seattle to New Orleans, a distance of 2,098 miles?

It would be _____ passenger-miles.

7. A tank truck made 275 trips in a year. It hauled 5,950 gallons each trip. How many gallons did it haul that year?

It hauled _____ gallons.

8. Suppose the truck in problem 7 hauled 8,725 gallons each trip. How many gallons would it haul?

It would haul _____ gallons.

1.	2.
3.	4.
5.	6.
7.	8.

Perfect score: 8   My score: _____

24

CHAPTER 2 TEST

Multiply.

	a	b	c	d
1.	31 ×3	25 ×3	276 ×6	583 ×7
2.	23 ×13	42 ×26	38 ×17	53 ×45
3.	123 ×31	425 ×70	563 ×25	837 ×85
4.	213 ×132	421 ×378	256 ×108	845 ×374
5.	1221 ×312	1456 ×173	1827 ×570	3456 ×732

Perfect score: 20   My score: _____

PRE-TEST—Division

Divide.

	a	*b*	*c*	*d*
1.	7⟌6 3	6⟌5 4	5⟌7 5	4⟌9 2
2.	4⟌1 3 6	5⟌3 7 0	3⟌4 7 1	2⟌9 6 0
3.	3⟌1 5 3 9	4⟌3 6 7 2	7⟌7 1 0 5	5⟌8 6 0 5
4.	4⟌8 7	2⟌7 5	3⟌8 6	3⟌7 8 1
5.	6⟌1 4 3	4⟌9 2 2 6	2⟌1 4 3 5	5⟌6 1 3 4

Perfect score: 20   My score: _____

26

Lesson 1　Division

$$9 \dashrightarrow 9$$
$$\times 5 \dashrightarrow 5\overline{)45}$$
$$\overline{45} \dashrightarrow$$

$$9 \dashrightarrow 5$$
$$\times 5 \dashrightarrow 9\overline{)45}$$
$$\overline{45}$$

If $5 \times 9 = 45$, then $45 \div 5 = 9$ and $45 \div 9 = 5$.

Divide.

	a	b	c	d	e	f
1.	$2\overline{)6}$	$3\overline{)9}$	$2\overline{)4}$	$2\overline{)8}$	$3\overline{)6}$	$4\overline{)8}$
2.	$1\overline{)5}$	$3\overline{)3}$	$6\overline{)0}$	$1\overline{)9}$	$2\overline{)2}$	$7\overline{)7}$
3.	$4\overline{)28}$	$6\overline{)42}$	$3\overline{)18}$	$6\overline{)36}$	$8\overline{)32}$	$2\overline{)14}$
4.	$2\overline{)10}$	$8\overline{)72}$	$7\overline{)42}$	$5\overline{)20}$	$3\overline{)15}$	$4\overline{)36}$
5.	$8\overline{)24}$	$2\overline{)18}$	$1\overline{)8}$	$4\overline{)32}$	$5\overline{)25}$	$9\overline{)81}$
6.	$7\overline{)35}$	$9\overline{)27}$	$6\overline{)24}$	$7\overline{)49}$	$8\overline{)48}$	$9\overline{)36}$
7.	$5\overline{)40}$	$3\overline{)24}$	$2\overline{)16}$	$6\overline{)48}$	$7\overline{)28}$	$9\overline{)54}$
8.	$5\overline{)15}$	$4\overline{)12}$	$2\overline{)12}$	$3\overline{)0}$	$6\overline{)54}$	$3\overline{)27}$
9.	$4\overline{)20}$	$8\overline{)56}$	$6\overline{)30}$	$4\overline{)24}$	$3\overline{)21}$	$5\overline{)30}$
10.	$8\overline{)16}$	$5\overline{)35}$	$4\overline{)16}$	$8\overline{)64}$	$9\overline{)63}$	$8\overline{)40}$

Perfect score: 60　　My score: _____

27

Problem Solving

Solve each problem.

1. There are 18 chairs and 6 tables in the room. There are the same number of chairs at each table. How many chairs are at each table?

There are _____ chairs.

There are _____ tables.

There are _____ chairs at each table.

2. Each box takes 3 minutes to fill. It took 18 minutes to fill all the boxes. How many boxes are there?

It takes _____ minutes to fill all the boxes.

It takes _____ minutes to fill 1 box.

There are _____ boxes.

3. Bob, Joe, Pete, Tom, Dick, and Jim share 6 sandwiches. How many sandwiches does each boy get?

There are _____ sandwiches in all.

The sandwiches are shared among _____ boys.

Each boy gets _____ sandwich.

4. Bill and 8 friends each sold the same number of tickets. They sold 72 tickets in all. How many tickets were sold by each person?

Each person sold _____ tickets.

5. Forty-eight oranges are in a crate. The oranges are to be put into bags of 6 each. How many bags can be filled?

_____ bags could be filled.

6. Jim has a wire that is 42 inches long. He cuts the wire into 7-inch lengths. How many pieces of wire will he have?

He will have _____ pieces of wire.

| 1. |
| 2. |
| 3. |
| 4. |
| 5. |
| 6. |

Perfect score: 12   My score: _____

28

Lesson 2   Division

Study how to divide 738 by 3.

X	100	200	300
3	300	600	900

X	10	20	30	40	50
3	30	60	90	120	150

X	1	2	3	4	5	6
3	3	6	9	12	15	18

738 is between 600 and 900, so $738 \div 3$ is between 200 and 300. The hundreds digit is 2.

```
  2
3)738
  600    (200×3)
  138    Subtract.
```

138 is between 120 and 150, so $138 \div 3$ is between 40 and 50. The tens digit is 4.

```
  24
3)738
  600
  138
  120    (40×3)
   18    Subtract.
```

$18 \div 3 = 6$, so the ones digit is 6.

```
   246
3)738
  600
  138
  120
   18
   18    (6×3)
```
remainder (r) --→ 0   Subtract.

Divide.

	a	b	c	d	e
1.	8)96	4)72	6)72	3)81	4)68
2.	2)74	3)87	5)75	7)784	3)768
3.	8)296	9)315	6)252	6)462	5)930

Problem Solving

Solve each problem.

1. There are 84 scouts in all. Six will be assigned to each tent. How many tents are there?

There are _____ scouts in all.

There are _____ scouts in each tent.

There are _____ tents.

2. Seven people each worked the same number of hours. They worked 91 hours in all. How many hours were worked by each person?

_____ hours were worked.

_____ people worked these hours.

_____ hours were worked by each person.

3. A group of three is a trio. How many trios could be formed with 72 people?

_____ trios could be formed.

4. A factory shipped 848 cars to 4 cities. Each city received the same number of cars. How many cars were shipped to each city?

_____ cars were shipped.

_____ cities received the cars.

_____ cars were shipped to each city.

5. Malcolm, his brother, and sister have 702 stamps in all. Suppose each takes the same number of stamps. How many will each get?

Each will get _____ stamps.

6. There are 6 outs in an inning. How many innings would have to be played to get 348 outs?

_____ innings would have to be played.

1.	2.
3.	4.
5.	6.

Perfect score: 12   My score: _____

30

Lesson 3   Division

Study how to divide 854 by 4.

X	100	200	300
4	400	800	1200

854

$854 \div 4$ is between 200 and 300. The hundreds digit is 2.

```
   2
4|854
  800     (200×4)
  ___
   54     Subtract.
```

X	10	20	30	40
4	40	80	120	160

54

$54 \div 4$ is between 10 and 20. The tens digit is 1.

```
  21
4|854
  800
  ___
   54
   40     (10×4)
   ___
   14     Subtract.
```

X	1	2	3	4	5
4	4	8	12	16	20

14

$14 \div 4$ is between 3 and 4. The ones digit is 3.

```
  213 r2
4|854
  800
  ___
   54
   40
   ___
   14
   12     (3×4)
   ___
    2     Subtract.
```

Divide.

	a	b	c	d	e
1.	3)82	5)86	4)97	3)76	2)47
2.	7)83	5)69	6)224	4)127	2)380
3.	4)231	5)653	7)962	2)483	6)832

Perfect score: 15   My score: _____

Problem Solving

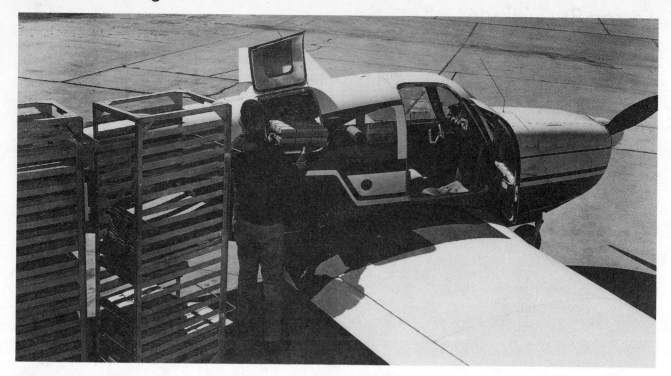

Solve each problem.

1. There are 160 packages on 4 large carts. Each cart holds the same number of packages. How many packages are on each cart?

Each cart has _____ packages.

1.

2. There are 160 packages. To deliver most of the packages, it will take 3 small planes. Each plane will take the same number of packages. How many packages will each plane take? How many packages will be left over?

Each plane will take _____ packages.

There will be _____ packages left over.

2.

3. Suppose there had been 890 packages to be delivered by 6 planes. Each plane is to take the same number of packages and as many as possible. How many packages will each plane take? How many will be left over?

Each plane will take _____ packages.

There will be _____ packages left over.

3.

Perfect score: 5   My score: _____

Lesson 4   Division

```
    235                              178 r2
  8|1880  ←                        3|536  ←
   1600        These     Check      300        These     Check
   ────        should              ────        should
    280        be the     235       236        be the     178
    240        same.      ×8        210        same.      ×3
   ────                  ────      ────                  ────
     40        →        1880        26                   534
     40                              24                   +2
   ────                            ────                  ────
      0                               2        →          536
```

To check $1880 \div 8 = 235$,
   multiply 235 by 8. The answer should be _____.
To check $536 \div 3 = 178$ r2,
   multiply 178 by 3 and then add 2. The answer should be _____.

Divide. Check each answer.

         a   *b*   *c*

1. $4\overline{)1104}$ $8\overline{)1760}$ $2\overline{)4632}$

2. $3\overline{)379}$ $5\overline{)421}$ $4\overline{)762}$

3. $3\overline{)1058}$ $6\overline{)726}$ $7\overline{)2117}$

Perfect score: 9   My score: _____

Problem Solving

Solve each problem. Check each answer.

1. How many bags of 7 oranges each can be filled from a shipment of 341 oranges? How many oranges will be left over?

_____ bags can be filled.

_____ oranges will be left over.

2. Beverly has $2.38 (238 cents) to buy pencils for 8¢ each. How many pencils can she buy? How many cents will she have left?

She can buy _____ pencils.

She will have _____ cents left.

3. There are 6 stamps in each row. How many complete rows can be filled with 1,950 stamps? How many stamps will be left over?

_____ rows will be filled.

_____ stamps will be left over.

4. Daphne had 958 pennies. She exchanged them for nickels. How many nickels did she get? How many pennies did she have left over?

She got _____ nickels.

She had _____ pennies left over.

5. Last year Mr. Gomez worked 1,983 hours. How many 8-hour days was this? How many hours are left over?

It was _____ 8-hour days.

_____ hours are left over.

6. There are 7,633 points to be divided among Paul, Fred, and Leroy. Each boy is to receive the same number of points. How many points will each receive? How many points will be left over?

Each boy will receive _____ points.

_____ points will be left over.

| **1.** |
| **2.** |
| **3.** |
| **4.** |
| **5.** |
| **6.** |

Perfect score: 12   My score: _____

CHAPTER 3 TEST

Divide.

	a	b	c	d
1.	4⟌9 6	7⟌8 4	3⟌7 9	5⟌6 8
2.	4⟌7 3 2	5⟌1 7 5	7⟌6 1 5	2⟌6 4 7
3.	8⟌1 7 2 0	4⟌5 2 1 6	4⟌1 5 3 0	3⟌6 3 2 3
4.	3⟌8 4	6⟌7 6	8⟌9 4	2⟌7 8
5.	4⟌1 2 5 6	3⟌6 3 4 3	5⟌1 8 4 2	6⟌7 2 0 6

Perfect score: 20   My score: _____

PRE-TEST—Division

Divide.

	a	*b*	*c*	*d*

1. 13⟌7 8 14⟌9 8 12⟌6 5 15⟌9 5

2. 24⟌3 1 2 37⟌9 6 2 12⟌5 8 6 23⟌5 5 0

3. 27⟌3 5 6 4 74⟌7 2 5 2 36⟌2 0 2 6 34⟌3 8 3 0

4. 16⟌7 6 8 52⟌2 7 2 4 18⟌3 1 0 14⟌5 6

5. 34⟌4 2 8 4 53⟌2 1 2 0 26⟌9 6 4 11⟌4 1 8

Perfect score: 20   My score: _____

Lesson 1 Division

Study how to divide 94 by 13.

Since $10 \times 13 = 130$ and 130 is greater than 94, there is no tens digit.

$13\overline{)94}$

X	1	2	3	4	5	6	7	8
13	13	26	39	52	65	78	91	104

94 is between 91 and 104.
$94 \div 13$ is between 7 and 8.
The *quotient* is 7.

```
        7
  13)94
     91    (7 × 13)
    ───
      3    (94 − 91)
```

Record the remainder like this.

```
        7 r3
  13)94        ↑
     91        remainder
    ───
      3
```

Divide.

	a	b	c	d	e
1.	$12\overline{)84}$	$13\overline{)78}$	$19\overline{)95}$	$16\overline{)84}$	$14\overline{)98}$
2.	$15\overline{)92}$	$14\overline{)75}$	$16\overline{)74}$	$13\overline{)80}$	$12\overline{)92}$
3.	$17\overline{)68}$	$23\overline{)92}$	$32\overline{)84}$	$18\overline{)72}$	$27\overline{)91}$

Perfect score: 15   My score: _____

Problem Solving

Solve each problem.

1. The pet store has 84 birds. They have 14 large cages. There are the same number of birds in each cage. How many birds are in each cage?

_____ birds are in each cage.

2. The pet store also has 63 kittens. There are 12 cages with the same number of kittens in each. The rest of the kittens are in the display window. How many kittens are in each cage? How many kittens are in the display window?

_____ kittens are in each cage.

_____ kittens are in the display window.

3. There are 60 guppies in a large tank. If the pet store puts 15 guppies each in a smaller tank, how many smaller tanks will be needed?

_____ smaller tanks will be needed.

4. There are 72 boxes of pet food on a shelf. The boxes are in rows of 13 each. How many full rows of boxes are there? How many boxes are left over?

There are _____ full rows of boxes.

There are _____ boxes left over.

5. There are 80 cages to be cleaned. Each of the store's 19 employees is to clean the same number of cages. The owner will clean any leftover cages. How many cages will each employee clean? How many cages will the owner clean?

Each employee will clean _____ cages.

The owner will clean _____ cages.

6. There are 52 puppies. There are 13 cages. If each cage contains the same number of puppies, how many puppies are in each cage?

There are _____ puppies in each cage.

1.

2.

3.

4.

5.

6.

Perfect score: 9   My score: _____

38

Lesson 2 Division

Study how to divide 219 by 12.

X	10	20	30	40
12	120	240	360	480

219

$219 \div 12$ is between 10 and 20.
The tens digit is 1.

```
      1
12)219
   120
    99
```

X	1	2	3	4	5	6	7	8	9
12	12	24	36	48	60	72	84	96	108

99

$99 \div 12$ is between 8 and 9.
The ones digit is 8.

```
      18 r3
12)219
   120
    99
    96
     3
```

Divide.

	a	*b*	*c*	*d*	*e*
1.	13)3 5 1	16)2 5 6	17)3 2 3	14)4 9 0	12)8 1 4
2.	26)3 1 6	31)4 1 3	17)2 1 2	24)3 6 0	28)5 6 4

Perfect score: 10   My score: _____

39

Problem Solving

Solve each problem.

1. There are 448 reams of paper in the supply room. Fourteen reams are used each day. At that rate, how many days will the supply of paper last?

The supply of paper will last _____ days.

2. There are 338 cases on a truck. The truck will make 12 stops and leave the same number of cases at each stop. How many cases will be left at each stop? How many cases will still be on the truck?

_____ cases will be left at each stop.

_____ cases will still be on the truck.

3. There are 582 tickets to be sold. Each of 24 pupils is to receive the same number of tickets and as many as possible. The teacher is to sell any tickets left over. How many tickets is each pupil to sell? How many is the teacher to sell?

Each pupil is to sell _____ tickets.

The teacher is to sell _____ tickets.

4. A machine operated 38 hours and produced 988 parts. The same number of parts was produced each hour. How many parts were produced each hour?

_____ parts are produced each hour.

5. After 24 hours, the machine in problem 4 had produced 582 parts. About how many parts is the machine producing each hour? Is it producing at the rate it is designed to do?

About _____ parts are being produced each hour.

The machine _____ producing as designed.

6. Suppose the machine in problem 4 was operated 19 hours. During this time 988 parts were produced. The same number of parts was produced each hour. How many were produced each hour?

_____ parts are produced each hour.

1.
2.
3.
4.
5.
6.

Perfect score: 9   My score: _____

40

Lesson 3   Division

```
      8 r2                                    Check      8
  12⟌98                                               × 12
    96          These should                            16
     2          be the same.                            80
                                                        96
                                                       + 2
                                                        98
```

To check $98 \div 12 = 8$ r2, multiply 8

by _____ and add _____ to that product.

The answer should be _____.

```
        12                                    Check     12
  34⟌408                                              × 34
   340          These should                           48
    68          be the same.                          360
    68                                                408
     0
```

To check $408 \div 34 = 12$, multiply 12

by _____. The answer should be _____.

Divide. Check each answer.

	a	b	c
1.	16⟌88	14⟌84	23⟌94
2.	19⟌114	36⟌756	32⟌836
3.	25⟌330	36⟌672	45⟌810

Perfect score: 9   My score: _____

41

Problem Solving

Solve each problem. Check each answer.

1. Lucinda had 59 cents to buy pencils that cost 14 cents each. How many pencils could she buy? How many cents would she have left over?

She could buy _____ pencils.

She would have _____ cents left.

2. The grocer has 98 cans of beans to put on a shelf. He thinks he can put 16 cans in each row. If he does, how many rows will he have? How many cans will be left over?

He will have _____ rows.

_____ cans will be left over.

3. The grocer in problem **2** could only put 13 cans in each row. How many rows does he have? How many cans are left over?

He has _____ rows.

_____ cans are left over.

4. There are 774 cartons ready for shipment. Only 27 cartons can be shipped on each truck. How many full truckloads will there be? How many cartons will be left?

There will be _____ full loads.

_____ cartons will be left.

5. There are 605 books in the storage room. There are the same number of books in each of 17 full boxes and the rest in an extra box. How many books are in each full box? How many books are in the extra box?

_____ books are in each full box.

_____ books are in the extra box.

1.

2.

3.

4.

5.

Perfect score: 10   My score: _____

42

Lesson 4   Division

Study how to divide 8550 by 25.

X	100	200	300	400
25	2500	5000	7500	10000

8550

The hundreds digit is 3.

```
     3
25 | 8550
   7500
   1050
```

X	10	20	30	40	50
25	250	500	750	1000	1250

1050

The tens digit is 4.

```
    34
25 | 8550
   7500
   1050
   1000
     50
```

X	1	2
25	25	50

50

The ones digit is 2.

```
    342
25 | 8550
   7500
   1050
   1000
     50
     50
      0
```

Divide.

	a	b	c	d
1.	32) 5 2 8 0	43) 6 7 5 1	26) 6 3 1 8	75) 9 1 5 0
2.	42) 8 9 5 6	31) 9 8 7 5	23) 3 8 4 4	63) 9 0 0 8
3.	35) 1 9 6 0	75) 3 9 0 0	63) 2 6 5 6	27) 1 4 3 0

Perfect score: 12   My score: _____

Problem Solving

Solve each problem.

1. A truck is loaded with 8,073 kilograms of food. Each case of food weighs 23 kilograms. How many cases are on the truck?

_____ cases are on the truck.

2. During an 8-hour shift, one machine was able to package 8,215 boxes of rice. These boxes were packed 24 to a carton. How many full cartons of rice would this be? How many boxes would be left over?

There would be _____ full cartons.

_____ boxes would be left over.

3. The bakery uses 75 pounds of butter in each batch of butter-bread dough. How many batches of dough could be made with 6,300 pounds of butter?

_____ batches of dough could be made.

4. There are 2,030 pupils in school. How many classes of 28 pupils each could there be? How many pupils would be left over?

There could be _____ full classes.

_____ pupils would be left over.

5. In 27 days 3,888 gallons of oil were used. The same amount of oil was used each day. How much oil was used each day?

_____ gallons were used each day.

6. There were 5,100 parts to be packed. The parts are to be packed 24 to a box. How many boxes can be filled? How many parts would be left over?

_____ full boxes can be packed.

_____ parts would be left over.

1.	
2.	
3.	
4.	
5.	
6.	

Perfect score: 9   My score: _____

44

Lesson 5   Division

Divide.

	a	b	c	d

1. 28)7 7 6   42)5 1 7 6   19)9 5   33)1 3 3

(c) handwritten: 4 20 100 5 ... 95

(d) handwritten: 4 01 ... 132 ... 00 1

2. 12)2 6 0 6   22)6 7 5 4   24)7 9 2   11)1 7 1 6

(b) handwritten: 307 ... -66 ... 15 ... 0 ... 154 ... -154

(c) handwritten: 33 ... -72 ... 072 ... -72 ... 00

(d) handwritten: 156 ... 11 ... 5 1 ... -55 ... 66 ... -66 ... 0

3. 14)8 4   89)8 0 1   75)7 5 3   16)2 6 1 6

4. 75)6 3 7 5   23)5 5 4 3   25)8 0 0 0   25)8 0 0

5. 15)6 0 0 9   60)1 8 6 0   20)7 0 2 0   48)1 7 0 4

Perfect score: 20   My score: _____

Problem Solving

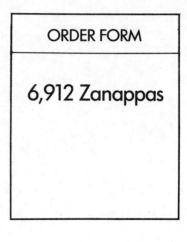

ORDER FORM
6,912 Zanappas

Solve each problem.

1. An order was received for 6,912 zanappas. Machine A can produce the zanappas in 12 hours. At that rate, how many zanappas would be produced each hour?

_____ zanappas would be produced each hour.

2. It would take machine B 24 hours to produce the zanappas needed to fill the order. At that rate, how many zanappas would be produced each hour?

_____ zanappas would be produced each hour.

3. Machine C could produce the zanappas needed to fill the order in 48 hours. At that rate, how many zanappas could be produced each hour?

_____ zanappas could be produced each hour.

4. How many zanappas could be produced if all three machines operated for a period of 8 hours?

_____ zanappas could be produced.

1.

2.

3.

4.

Perfect score: 4   My score: _____

46

CHAPTER 4 TEST

Divide.

	a	b	c	d
	a	*b*	*c*	*d*

1. 12)7 2   13)8 9   11)9 4   17)6 8

2. 17)2 6 5   11)8 5 8   31)9 6 1   12)5 0 6

3. 36)4 3 6 6   42)1 8 9 0   73)3 9 3 4   14)2 1 8 4

4. 13)1 6 9   26)3 1 7 5   16)7 5   36)1 4 4

5. 54)1 4 5 8   25)2 0 9 5   28)5 7 3   42)9 9

Perfect score: 20   My score: _____

PRE-TEST—Division

Divide.

	a	*b*	*c*	*d*
1.	25)7 5	25)7 5 0	25)7 5 0 0	25)7 5 0 0 0
2.	38)4 2 5 6 0	17)4 0 3 3 9	33)7 3 3 2 6	25)2 1 4 5 0
3.	42)8 9 5 2 3	16)9 7 9 7 8	25)6 2 9 4 0	15)3 1 7 6 2
4.	27)1 2 2 0 4	48)2 7 6 4 8	62)1 9 6 6 4	72)3 1 9 6 8

Perfect score: 16   My score: _____

48

Lesson 1 Division

Study how to divide 24567 by 12.

X	1000	2000	3000
12	12000	24000	36000

24567

The thousands digit is 2.

```
        2
  12│24567
     24000
       567
```

X	100	200
12	1200	2400

567 ÷ 12 is less than 100. The hundreds digit is 0.

```
       20
  12│24567
     24000
       567
```

X	30	40	50
12	360	480	600

567

The tens digit is 4.

```
      204
  12│24567
     24000
       567
       480
        87
```

X	6	7	8
12	72	84	96

87

The ones digit is 7.

```
      2047 r3
  12│24567
     24000
       567
       480
        87
        84
         3
```

Divide.

	a	b	c	d
1.	36│4500	26│8430	92│7911	25│3575
2.	24│77184	92│39754	56│69104	23│17342

Perfect score: 8   My score: _____

49

Problem Solving

Solve each problem.

1. In 27 days, 6,939 orders were filled. The same number of orders was filled each day. How many orders were filled each day?

_____ orders were filled each day.

2. Yesterday 5,650 school children came in buses to visit the museum. How many full bus loads of pupils were there if 75 pupils make up a full load? How many pupils were on the partially filled bus?

There were _____ full bus loads.

_____ pupils were on the partially filled bus.

3. The inventory slip shows that there are 7,840 pairs of stockings in the warehouse. There are 32 pairs in each box. How many boxes of stockings should there be in the warehouse?

There should be _____ boxes of stockings.

4. A factory produced 7,605 zimbits yesterday. The zimbits are packed 24 to a box. How many full boxes of zimbits were produced? How many zimbits were left over?

It was _____ full boxes.

_____ zimbits are left over.

5. The grandstand is separated into 16 sections. Each section has the same number of seats. There are 8,640 seats in all. How many seats are in each section?

There are _____ seats in each section.

6. Suppose there were 9,600 seats in the grandstand in problem 5. How many seats would be in each section?

There would be _____ seats in each section.

1.

2.

3.

4.

5.

6.

Perfect score: 8   My score: _____

50

Lesson 2   Division

Study how to divide 24205 by 75.

X	100	200	300	400
75	7500	15000	22500	30000

24205

The hundreds digit is 3.

```
     3
75)24205
   22500
    1705
```

X	10	20	30	40
75	750	1500	2250	3000

1705

The tens digit is 2.

```
    32
75)24205
   22500
    1705
    1500
     205
```

X	1	2	3	4
75	75	150	225	300

205

The ones digit is 2.

```
    322 r55
75)24205
   22500
    1705
    1500
     205
     150
      55
```

Divide.

	a	b	c	d
1.	43)17716	64)32768	27)22005	28)60088
2.	33)27313	31)96843	43)89800	59)41645

Perfect score: 8   My score: _____

51

Problem Solving

Solve each problem.

1. A bus can carry 86 passengers. How many such buses would be needed to carry 20,898 passengers?

_____ buses would be needed.

2. There are 16 ounces in one pound. How many pounds are there in 39,238 ounces? How many ounces are left over?

There are _____ pounds.

There are _____ ounces left over.

3. There are 31,500 pounds of salt to be put into bags with 58 pounds in each bag. How many full bags of salt would there be? How many pounds would be left over?

There would be _____ full bags.

_____ pounds would be left over.

4. It takes 72 hours for one machine to produce 14,616 parts. The machine produces the same number of parts each hour. How many parts does it produce each hour?

It produces _____ parts each hour.

5. Suppose the machine in problem 4 could produce the parts in 36 hours. How many parts would it produce each hour?

It would produce _____ parts each hour.

6. Suppose the machine in problem 4 could produce the parts in 18 hours. How many parts would it produce each hour?

It would produce _____ parts each hour.

7. Suppose the machine in problem 4 could produce the parts in 12 hours. How many parts would it produce each hour?

It would produce _____ parts each hour.

1.

2.

3.

4.

5.

6.

7.

Perfect score: 9   My score: _____

52

Lesson 3   Division

```
        2543 r8         Check
   16|40696             2543
      32000            × 16
   ───────            ──────
       8696     These  15258
       8000    should  25430
   ───────     be the  ──────
        696    same.   40688
        640              + 8
   ───────            ──────
         56            40696
         48
   ───────
          8
```

To check 40696 ÷ 16 = 2543 r8, multiply

2543 by _____ and then add _____ to this

product. The answer should be _____.

Divide. Check each answer.

         a   *b*

1. 47|9 9 9 3 2   54|3 3 1 0 0

2. 38|2 7 5 9 0   46|3 8 2 7 7

3. 75|9 5 1 0 0   24|3 0 9 0 0

Perfect score: 6   My score: _____

Problem Solving

Solve each problem. Check each answer.

1. There are 35 gates into the stadium and 15,330 people attended the game. The same number entered through each gate. How many entered each gate?

_____ people entered each gate.

2. A garage used 16,434 liters of oil in 83 days. The same amount of oil was used each day. How much oil was used each day?

_____ liters were used each day.

3. During 6 months, 77 employees worked 67,639 hours. Suppose each employee worked the same number of hours. How many hours did each work? How many hours would be left over?

Each employee worked _____ hours.

_____ hours are left over.

4. Ninety-five containers of the same size were filled with a total of 82,840 kilograms of coal. How many kilograms of coal were in each container?

_____ kilograms were in each container.

5. There are 46,963 pupils attending 52 schools in the city. Suppose the same number attend each school. How many pupils would attend each school? How many would be left over?

_____ pupils would attend each school.

_____ pupils would be left over.

6. Suppose there were twice as many pupils in problem 5. How many pupils would attend each school? How many would be left over?

_____ pupils would attend each school.

_____ pupils would be left over.

1.

2.

3.

4.

5.

6.

Perfect score: 9   My score: _____

54

Lesson 4   Division

Divide.

	a	*b*	*c*	*d*

1.   38$\overline{)7\,2}$ 23$\overline{)6\,0\,1}$ 32$\overline{)4\,6\,4\,0}$ 34$\overline{)4\,3\,8\,7\,7}$

2.   24$\overline{)5\,4}$ 24$\overline{)5\,4\,0}$ 24$\overline{)5\,4\,0\,0}$ 24$\overline{)5\,4\,0\,0\,0}$

3.   12$\overline{)8\,7}$ 21$\overline{)1\,6\,8}$ 42$\overline{)1\,4\,9\,1}$ 38$\overline{)2\,1\,5\,8\,4}$

4.   87$\overline{)9\,5}$ 24$\overline{)3\,6\,9}$ 75$\overline{)6\,0\,0\,5}$ 45$\overline{)3\,0\,6\,0\,5}$

Perfect score: 16   My score: _____

Problem Solving

Solve each problem.

1. Paula is to read 228 pages in 4 sessions. She will read the same number of pages each session. How many pages will she read each session?

She will read _____ pages each session.

2. The square of a number is found by multiplying the number by itself. Harold said that 2,916 is the square of 54. Is he right?

Harold _____ right.

3. The astronauts are now 8,640 minutes into their flight. How many hours would this be? How many days?

It would be _____ hours.

It would be _____ days.

4. In five hours 15,190 cans came off the assembly line. There are 88 cans packed in each carton. How many full cartons are there? How many cans are in the partially filled carton?

There are _____ full cartons.

There are _____ cans in the partial carton.

5. A satellite has just completed its 94th orbit. It has been in orbit for 13,160 hours. How long does it take to make a complete orbit?

It takes _____ hours to make one orbit.

6. How long will the satellite in problem 5 be in orbit after it has completed its 100th orbit?

It will have been in orbit _____ hours.

1.

2.

3.

4.

5.

6.

Perfect score: 8   My score: _____

56

CHAPTER 5 TEST

Divide.

	a	b	c	d
1.	97)873	56)952	70)2870	63)6615
2.	31)8308	41)5043	11)1232	77)9831
3.	32)23744	93)31657	51)21483	43)31605
4.	25)23375	17)34096	37)65510	77)92324
5.	35)35035	25)10025	31)93006	13)10413

Perfect score: 20   My score: _____

PRE-TEST—Metric Measurement

Find the length of each line segment to the nearest centimeter (cm).
Then find the length of each line segment to the nearest millimeter (mm).

        a   *b*

1. _____ cm   _____ mm

2. _____ cm   _____ mm

Find the perimeter and the area of each rectangle.

3. *perimeter:* _____ centimeters

    area: _____ square centimeters

2 centimeters

3 centimeters

4. *perimeter:* _____ millimeters

    area: _____ square millimeters

15 millimeters

15 millimeters

Complete the following.

           a   *b*

5. 7 centimeters = _____ millimeters   28 meters = _____ centimeters

6. 9 meters = _____ centimeters   49 meters = _____ millimeters

7. 8 kilometers = _____ meters   16 liters = _____ milliliters

8. 5 kiloliters = _____ liters   5 kilograms = _____ grams

9. 2 grams = _____ milligrams   14 centimeters = _____ millimeters

10. 40 liters = _____ milliliters   42 meters = _____ centimeters

11. 3 kiloliters = _____ liters   35 meters = _____ millimeters

12. 60 kilograms = _____ grams   34 kilometers = _____ meters

Perfect score: 24   My score: _____

Lesson 1 Centimeter and Millimeter

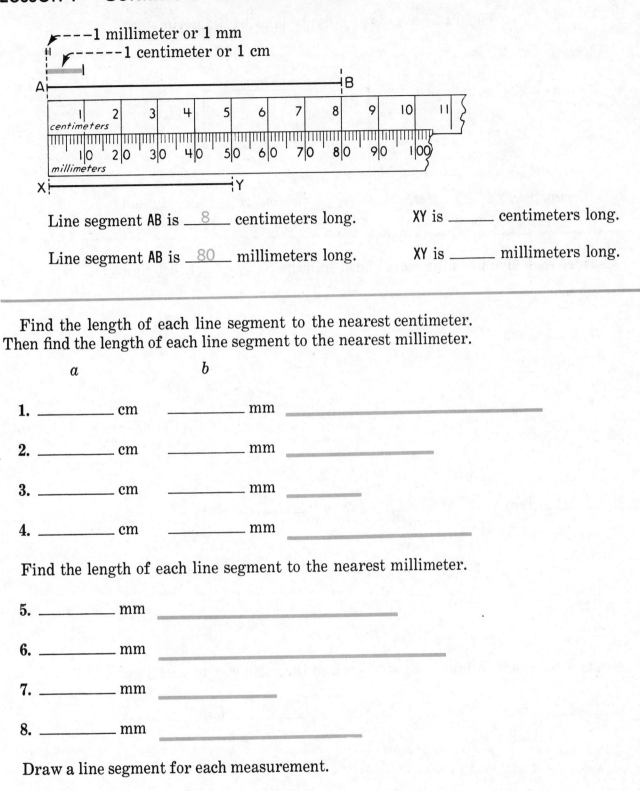

Line segment AB is __8__ centimeters long. XY is _____ centimeters long.

Line segment AB is __80__ millimeters long. XY is _____ millimeters long.

Find the length of each line segment to the nearest centimeter.
Then find the length of each line segment to the nearest millimeter.

     a   *b*

1. _____ cm   _____ mm

2. _____ cm   _____ mm

3. _____ cm   _____ mm

4. _____ cm   _____ mm

Find the length of each line segment to the nearest millimeter.

5. _____ mm

6. _____ mm

7. _____ mm

8. _____ mm

Draw a line segment for each measurement.

9. 6 cm

10. 45 mm

Perfect score: 14   My score: _____

Lesson 2 Perimeter

The distance around a figure is called its **perimeter.**

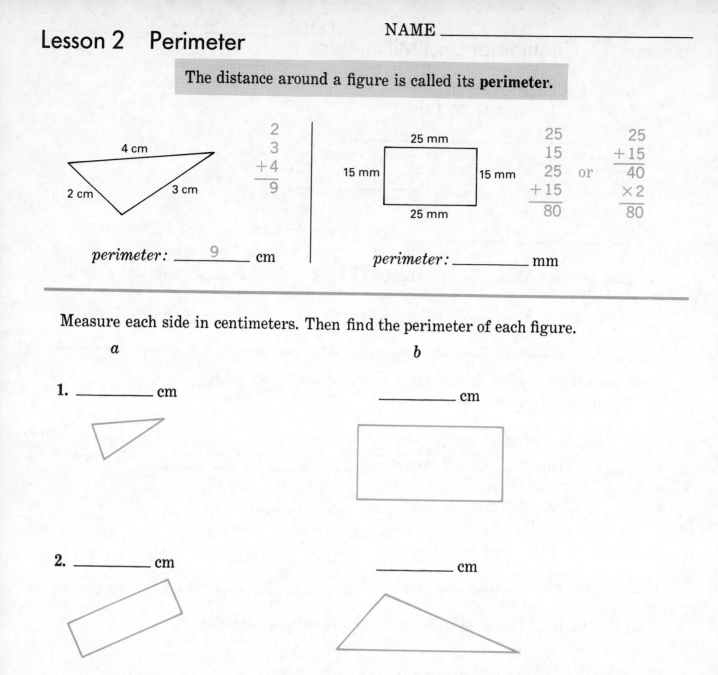

perimeter: _____9_____ cm

perimeter: _____ mm

Measure each side in centimeters. Then find the perimeter of each figure.

a

b

1. _____ cm

_____ cm

2. _____ cm

_____ cm

Measure each side in millimeters. Then find the perimeter of each figure.

3. _____ mm

_____ mm

Perfect score: 6   My score: _____

Lesson 3 Meter and Kilometer

A baseball bat is
about **1 meter** long.

1 meter (m) or 100 cm

| 1 m = 100 cm |
| 1 cm = .01 m |

If you run from goal line
to goal line on a football
field **11** times, you will
run about **1 kilometer**.

1000 meters is the same distance as 1 kilometer (km).

| 1 km = 1000 m |
| 1 m = .001 km |

Use a meter stick to find the following to the nearest meter.

    a   *b*

1. length of your room _____ m width of a door _____ m

2. width of your room _____ m width of a window _____ m

3. height of a door _____ m height of a window _____ m

Answer each question.

4. Michelle's height is 105 centimeters. Is she taller
or shorter than 1 meter?

She is _____ than 1 meter.

5. Are you taller or shorter than 1 meter?

I am _____ than 1 meter.

6. Roberta wants to swim 1 kilometer. How many
meters should she swim?

She should swim _____ meters.

7. Sung-Chi ran 1,500 meters. Leona ran 1 kilometer. Who ran farther? How much farther?

_____ ran _____ meters farther.

4.

5.

6.

7.

Perfect score: 11 My score: _____

Lesson 4   Units of Length

Study how to change from one metric unit to another.

9 km = __?__ m

1 km = 1000 m

9 km = (9 × 1000) m

9 km = _9000_ m

850 mm = __?__ cm

10 mm = 1 cm

850 mm = (850 ÷ 10) cm

850 mm = _____ cm

Complete the following.

          a

1. 50 km = _____ m

2. 70 mm = _____ cm

3. 9 cm = _____ mm

4. 3 m = _____ cm

          b

600 cm = _____ m

2000 mm = _____ m

8000 m = _____ km

5000 cm = _____ m

5. Ted is 4000 meters from school. Susan is 3 kilometers from school. How many meters from school is Susan? Who is farther from school? How much farther?

Susan is _____ meters from school.

_____ is _____ meters farther from school.

5.

6. Maria is 134 centimeters tall. Su-Lyn is 1300 millimeters tall. Charles is 141 centimeters tall. Who is tallest? Who is shortest?

_____ is tallest.

_____ is shortest.

6.

7. What is your height in centimeters? In millimeters?

I am _____ centimeters tall.

I am _____ millimeters tall.

7.

Perfect score: 15   My score: _____

Lesson 5 Area

> To find the **area** of a rectangle, multiply the measure of its length by the measure of its width.

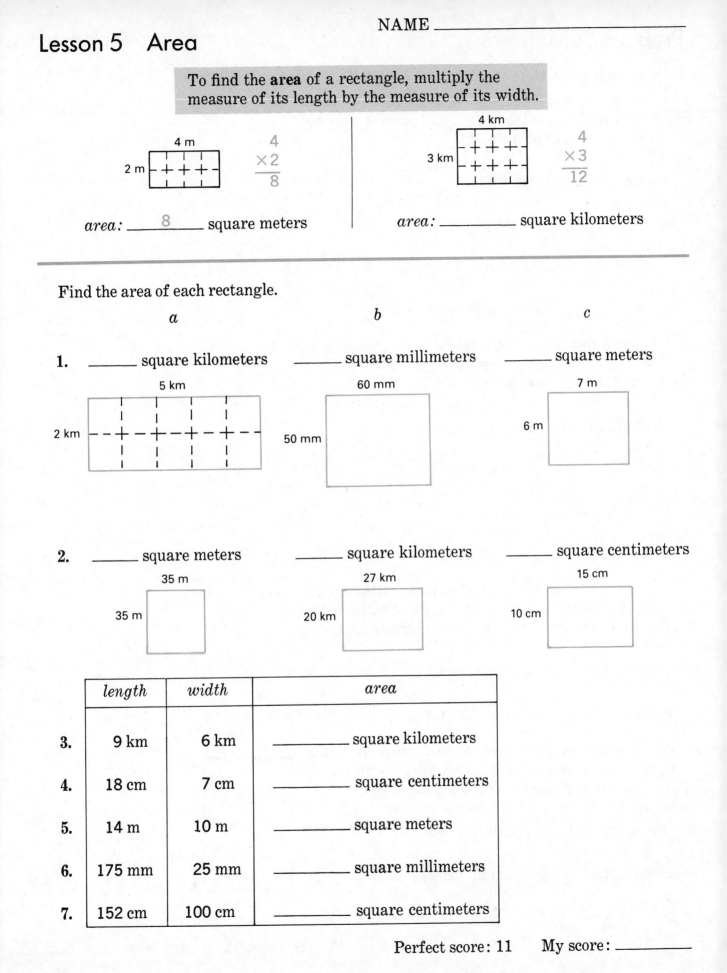

area: ___8___ square meters

area: _____ square kilometers

Find the area of each rectangle.

       a   *b*   *c*

1. _____ square kilometers   _____ square millimeters   _____ square meters

2. _____ square meters   _____ square kilometers   _____ square centimeters

	length	width	area
3.	9 km	6 km	_____ square kilometers
4.	18 cm	7 cm	_____ square centimeters
5.	14 m	10 m	_____ square meters
6.	175 mm	25 mm	_____ square millimeters
7.	152 cm	100 cm	_____ square centimeters

Perfect score: 11   My score: _____

Problem Solving

Solve each problem.

1. Find a rectangular room. Measure its length and width to the nearest meter. Find the perimeter of the room. Find the area of the room.

length: _____ meters

width: _____ meters

perimeter: _____ meters

area: _____ square meters

2. Find a rectangular tabletop or desk. Measure its length and width to the nearest meter. Find the perimeter of the top. Find the area of the top.

length: _____ meters

width: _____ meters

perimeter: _____ meters

area: _____ square meters

3. Use the front cover of this book. Measure its length and width to the nearest centimeter. Find the perimeter of the cover. Find the area of the front cover.

perimeter: _____ centimeters

area: _____ square centimeters

4. Use the rectangle at the right. Measure its length and width to the nearest millimeter. Find the perimeter of the rectangle. Find the area of the rectangle.

perimeter: _____ millimeters

area: _____ square millimeters

35 mm

24 mm

1.

2.

3.

4.

Perfect score: 12   My score: _____

64

Lesson 6 Capacity

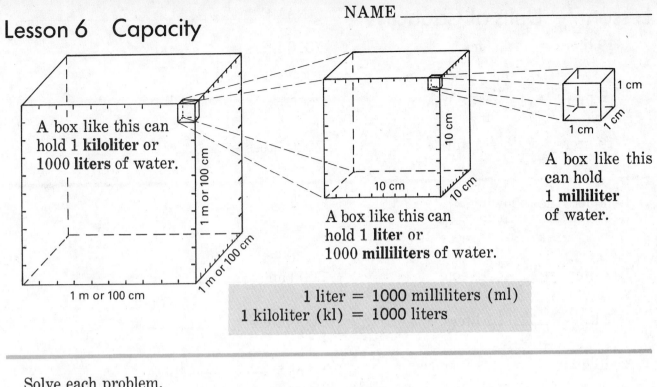

A box like this can hold 1 **kiloliter** or 1000 **liters** of water.

1 m or 100 cm

A box like this can hold 1 **liter** or 1000 **milliliters** of water.

10 cm   10 cm   10 cm

A box like this can hold 1 **milliliter** of water.

1 cm   1 cm   1 cm

1 liter = 1000 milliliters (ml)
1 kiloliter (kl) = 1000 liters

Solve each problem.

1. A teaspoon holds about 5 milliliters. A recipe calls for 2 teaspoons of vanilla. How many milliliters is that?

That is _____ milliliters.

2. A liter is slightly more than 4 cups. Do you drink more or less than a liter of milk every day?

I drink _____ than a liter every day.

3. To make punch, 8 cups of fruit juice are used. About how many liters would that be?

That would be _____ liters.

4. Two bathtubs filled with water would be about 1 kiloliter of water. Suppose your family uses 10 tubfuls of water a week. How many kiloliters of water would be used in a week?

_____ kiloliters would be used in a week.

5. A tank holds 1000 liters. How many kiloliters would it hold?

It would hold _____ kiloliter.

1.

2.

3.

4.

5.

Perfect score: 5   My score: _____

65

Lesson 7   Units of Capacity

19 liters = __?__ ml

1 liter = 1000 ml

19 liters = (19 × 1000) ml

19 liters = _19,000_ ml

7000 liters = __?__ kl

1000 liters = 1 kl

7000 liters = (7000 ÷ 1000) kl

7000 liters = _____ kl

Complete the following.

a   b

1. 7 liters = _____ ml   3000 ml = _____ liters

2. 2 kl = _____ liters   9000 liters = _____ kl

3. 20 liters = _____ ml   48 kl = _____ liters

4. 4000 ml = _____ liters   5000 liters = _____ kl

5. Lisa filled an ice-cube tray with water. Do you think she used about 1 *milliliter*, 1 *liter*, or 1 *kiloliter* of water?

She used 1 _____ of water.

5.

6. Carlos said he drank 500 milliliters of milk. Larry said he drank 1 liter of milk. Who drank more milk? How many milliliters more?

_____ drank _____ milliliters more milk.

6.

7. The gasoline tank on Mrs. Mohr's car holds 85 liters. It took 27 liters of fuel to fill the tank. How much fuel was in the tank before it was filled?

_____ liters were in the tank.

7.

8. A tank can hold 4000 liters of water. There are 3 kiloliters of water in the tank. How many liters of water are needed to fill the tank?

_____ liters are needed.

8.

Perfect score: 13   My score: _____

Lesson 8   Weight

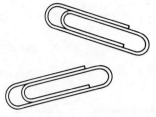

2 paper clips weigh
about **1 gram** (g).

3 new books like
yours weigh about
1 kilogram (kg).

1 gram = 1000 milligrams (mg)
1000 grams = 1 kilogram (kg)

Complete the following.

1. About how many grams do 4 paper clips weigh?

They weigh about _____ grams.

2. A box contains 4000 paper clips. How many kilograms do those paper clips weigh?

They weigh _____ kilograms.

3. One nickel weighs about 5 grams. A roll of 40 nickels would weigh about how many grams?

It would weigh _____ grams.

4. How many kilograms would 6 new books like yours weigh?

They would weigh _____ kilograms.

5. A doctor has 3000 milligrams of medicine. How many grams is that?

That is _____ grams.

6. A dog weighs 17,000 grams. How many kilograms is that?

That is _____ kilograms.

1.

2.

3.

4.

5.

6.

Perfect score: 6   My score: _____

Lesson 9   Units of Weight

6 kg = ___?___ g

   1 kg = 1000 g

   6 kg = (6 × 1000) g

     6 kg = _6000_ g

5000 mg = ___?___ g

   1000 mg = 1 g

   5000 mg = (5000 ÷ 1000) g

   5000 mg = _____ g

Complete the following.

        a   *b*

1. 2 kg = _____ g   6 g = _____ mg

2. 9 g = _____ mg   9 kg = _____ g

3. 2000 mg = _____ g   7000 g = _____ kg

4. 3000 g = _____ kg   8000 mg = _____ g

5. A penny weighs about 3 grams. A dime weighs about 2000 milligrams. Which weighs more? How much more?

   A _____ weighs about _____ milligrams more.

5.

6. Marta uses a 4-kilogram bowling ball. Her father uses a 7-kilogram bowling ball. How much heavier is her father's bowling ball?

   It is _____ kilograms heavier.

6.

7. A loaf of bread weighs 454 grams. How much would 3 loaves of bread weigh?

   They would weigh _____ grams.

7.

8. John weighs 34,000 grams. Judy weighs 39 kilograms. Who weighs more? How much more?

   _____ weighs _____ kilograms more.

8.

Perfect score: 14   My score: _____

CHAPTER 6 TEST

Find the length of each line segment to the nearest centimeter.
Then find the length of each line segment to the nearest millimeter.

a   b

1. _____ cm   _____ mm

2. _____ cm   _____ mm

Find the perimeter and the area of each rectangle.

3. *perimeter:* _____ meters   4. *perimeter:* _____ millimeters

   area: _____ square meters   *area:* _____ square millimeters

6 m   25 mm

4 m   15 mm

Complete the following.

a   b

5. 5 cm = _____ mm   2000 m = _____ km

6. 700 cm = _____ m   300 mm = _____ cm

7. 6 km = _____ m   3 m = _____ cm

8. 4 kl _____ liters   3000 ml = _____ liters

9. 2 liters = _____ ml   8 kg = _____ g

10. 7 g = _____ mg   5000 g = _____ kg

Perfect score: 20   My score: _____

69

Complete.

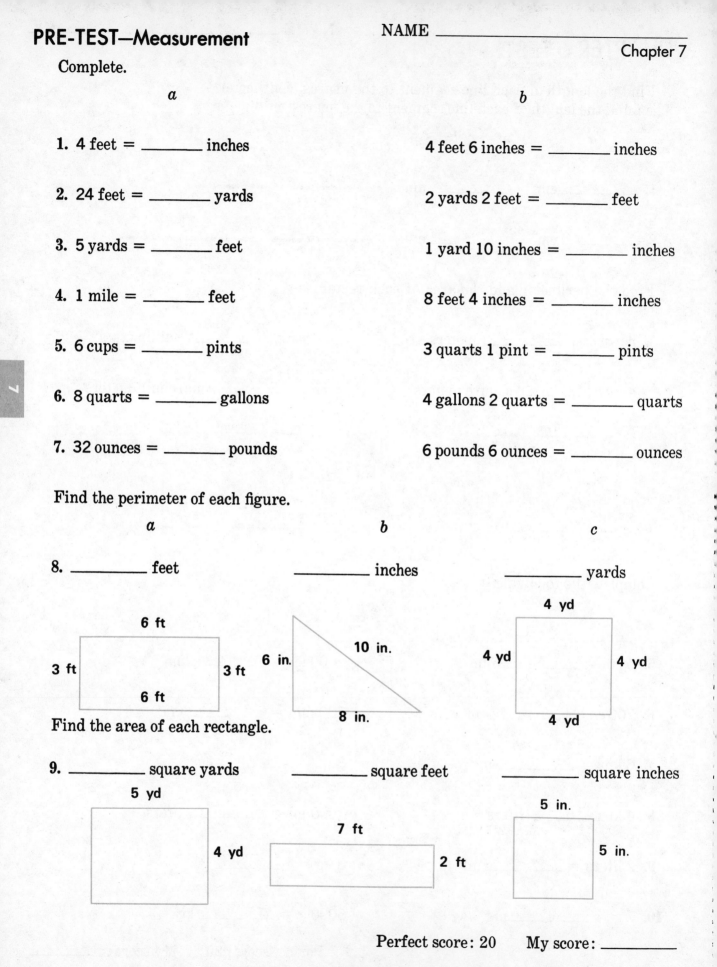

	a	b
1.	4 feet = _____ inches	4 feet 6 inches = _____ inches
2.	24 feet = _____ yards	2 yards 2 feet = _____ feet
3.	5 yards = _____ feet	1 yard 10 inches = _____ inches
4.	1 mile = _____ feet	8 feet 4 inches = _____ inches
5.	6 cups = _____ pints	3 quarts 1 pint = _____ pints
6.	8 quarts = _____ gallons	4 gallons 2 quarts = _____ quarts
7.	32 ounces = _____ pounds	6 pounds 6 ounces = _____ ounces

Find the perimeter of each figure.

 a   b   c

8. _____ feet   _____ inches   _____ yards

6 ft
3 ft   3 ft
6 ft

6 in.   10 in.
8 in.

4 yd
4 yd   4 yd
4 yd

Find the area of each rectangle.

9. _____ square yards   _____ square feet   _____ square inches

5 yd
4 yd

7 ft
2 ft

5 in.
5 in.

Perfect score: 20   My score: _____

70

Lesson 1   Units of Length

1 foot (ft) = 12 inches (in.)
1 mile (mi) = 5280 feet (ft)

1 yard (yd) = 3 ft
1 yard (yd) = 36 in.

24 in. = ____?____ ft

12 in. = 1 ft

24 in. = (24 ÷ 12) ft

24 in. = ___2___ ft

3 ft 4 in. = ____?____ in.

1 ft = 12 in.

3 ft = (3 × 12) or 36 in.

3 ft 4 in. = 36 in. + 4 in.

3 ft 4 in. = _____ in.

Complete the following.

	a	*b*
1.	6 ft = _____ in.	3 ft 2 in. = _____ in.
2.	2 yd = _____ in.	6 yd 11 in. = _____ in.
3.	3 mi = _____ ft	1 mi 450 ft = _____ ft
4.	84 in. = _____ ft	7 yd 1 ft = _____ ft
5.	180 in. = _____ yd	4 yd 7 in. = _____ in.
6.	15 ft = _____ yd	2 ft 6 in. = _____ in.

7. Becky threw the ball 24 yards. Wally threw the ball 840 inches. How many feet did each person throw the ball? Who threw it farther? How much farther?

Becky threw the ball _____ feet.

Wally threw the ball _____ feet.

_____ threw the ball _____ feet farther.

Perfect score: 16   My score: _____

Lesson 2   Perimeter

NAME _____

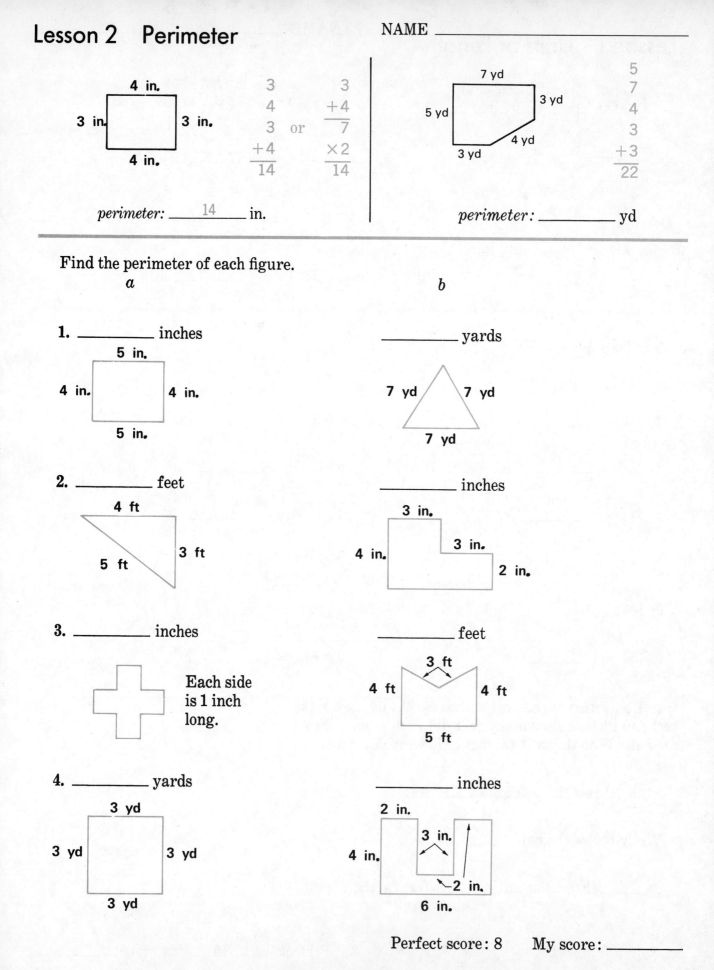

4 in.

3 in.   3 in.

4 in.

3
4
3
+4
—
14

or

3
+4
—
7

×2
—
14

perimeter: ___14___ in.

7 yd

5 yd   3 yd

3 yd   4 yd

5
7
4
3
+3
—
22

perimeter: _____ yd

Find the perimeter of each figure.

a

b

1. _____ inches

5 in.

4 in.   4 in.

5 in.

_____ yards

7 yd   7 yd

7 yd

2. _____ feet

4 ft

5 ft   3 ft

_____ inches

3 in.

3 in.

4 in.

2 in.

3. _____ inches

Each side is 1 inch long.

_____ feet

3 ft

4 ft   4 ft

5 ft

4. _____ yards

3 yd

3 yd   3 yd

3 yd

_____ inches

2 in.

3 in.

4 in.

2 in.

6 in.

Perfect score: 8   My score: _____

72

Lesson 3 Area

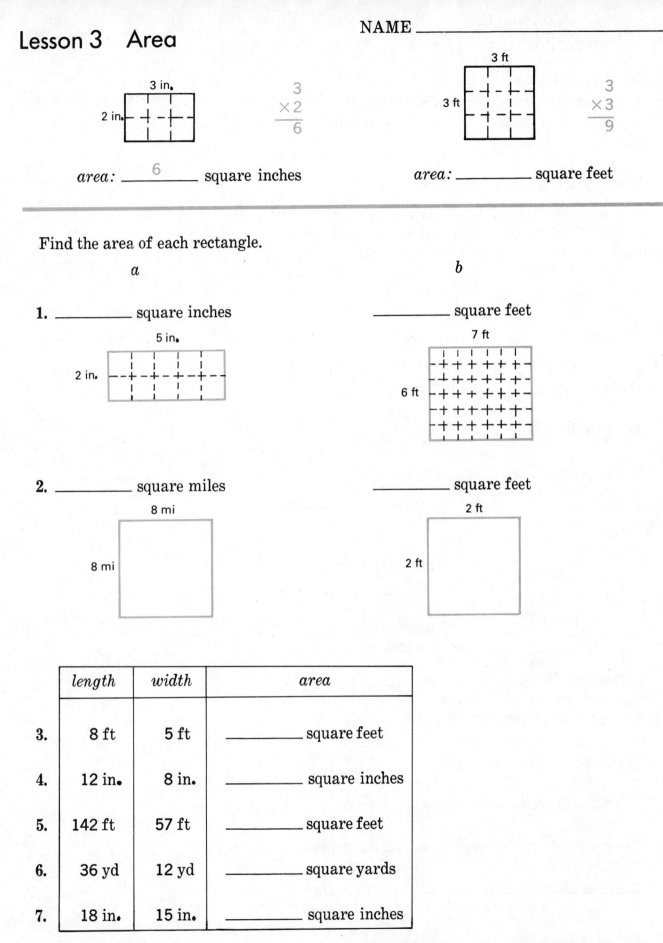

3 in.

2 in.

$$\begin{array}{r} 3 \\ \times 2 \\ \hline 6 \end{array}$$

area: ____6____ square inches

3 ft

3 ft

$$\begin{array}{r} 3 \\ \times 3 \\ \hline 9 \end{array}$$

area: _____ square feet

Find the area of each rectangle.

        a   *b*

1. _____ square inches   _____ square feet

5 in.

2 in.

7 ft

6 ft

2. _____ square miles   _____ square feet

8 mi

8 mi

2 ft

2 ft

	length	width	area
3.	8 ft	5 ft	_____ square feet
4.	12 in.	8 in.	_____ square inches
5.	142 ft	57 ft	_____ square feet
6.	36 yd	12 yd	_____ square yards
7.	18 in.	15 in.	_____ square inches

Perfect score: 9   My score: _____

Problem Solving

Solve each problem.

1. A garden has the shape of a rectangle. It is 24 feet long and 10 feet wide. What is the perimeter of the garden?

The perimeter is _____ feet.

2. A baseball diamond is a square with each side 90 feet long. Find the perimeter and the area of the diamond.

The perimeter is _____ feet.

The area is _____ square feet.

3. The square-shaped lot is 125 feet on each side. What is the perimeter of the lot? What is the area?

The perimeter is _____ feet.

The area is _____ square feet.

4. Find the perimeter and the area of the following figure.

The perimeter is _____ feet.

The area is _____ square feet.

5. Use the front cover of this book. Measure its length and its width to the nearest inch. Find the perimeter of the cover. Find the area of the cover.

The length of the cover is _____ inches.

The width of the cover is _____ inches.

The perimeter of the cover is _____ inches.

The area of the cover is _____ square inches.

1.	2.
3.	**4.**
5.	

Perfect score: 11   My score: _____

74

Lesson 4   Capacity and Weight

NAME _____

| 1 pint (pt) = 2 cups |
| 1 quart (qt) = 2 pt |

| 1 gallon (gal) = 4 qt |
| 1 pound (lb) = 16 ounces (oz) |

6 pt = ____?____ cups

1 pt = 2 cups

6 pt = (6 × 2) cups

6 pt = ___12___ cups

3 lb 4 oz = ____?____ oz

1 lb = 16 oz

3 lb = (3 × 16) oz
3 lb 4 oz = (48 + 4) oz

3 lb 4 oz = _____ oz

Complete the following.

a	*b*

1. 8 cups = _____ pt   1 lb 6 oz = _____ oz

2. 8 qt = _____ gal   6 lb 2 oz = _____ oz

3. 16 qt = _____ pt   3 qt 1 pt = _____ pt

4. 5 lb = _____ oz   6 gal 3 qt _____ qt

5. 15 pt = _____ cups   7 pt 1 cup = _____ cups

6. Terrance bought 6 pints of milk. He is going to give 1 cup of milk to each person. How many people can he serve?

He can serve _____ people.

6.

7. Mindy bought 6 pints of fruit juice. Sallie bought 1 gallon 1 quart of fruit juice. How many quarts of fruit juice did each person buy? Who bought more? How many quarts more?

Mindy bought _____ quarts.

Sallie bought _____ quarts.

_____ bought _____ quarts more.

7.

Perfect score: 15   My score: _____

75

Problem Solving

Solve each problem.

1. A fruit-drink recipe calls for 16 cups of water. How many pints of water is this? How many quarts?

It is _____ pints of water.

It is _____ quarts of water.

2. Ross counted 7 gallons of milk and 3 quarts of milk in the cooler. How many quarts of milk was this? How many pints of milk was this?

It was _____ quarts of milk.

It was _____ pints of milk.

3. Ann has 12 quarts and 1 pint of fruit drink. How many people can she serve at 1 pint per person? How many people can she serve at 1 cup per person?

She can serve _____ people at 1 pint each.

She can serve _____ people at 1 cup each.

4. Bernice and Charles have 3 pounds 12 ounces of hamburger. How many ounces is that?

That is _____ ounces.

5. How many 4-ounce hamburgers can be made from the meat in problem 4?

_____ 4-ounce hamburgers can be made.

6. How many 3-ounce hamburgers can be made from the meat in problem 4?

_____ 3-ounce hamburgers can be made.

7. How many 6-ounce hamburgers can be made from the meat in problem 4?

_____ 6-ounce hamburgers can be made.

1.

2.

3.

4.

5.

6.

7.

Perfect score: 10   My score: _____

76

CHAPTER 7 TEST

Complete the following.

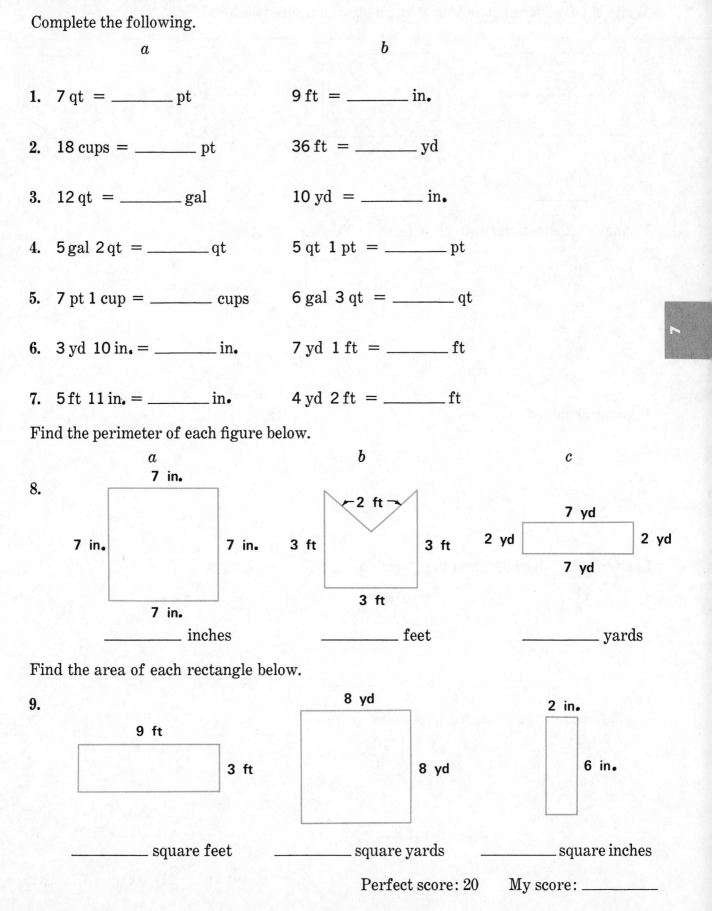

	a	*b*
1.	7 qt = _____ pt	9 ft = _____ in.
2.	18 cups = _____ pt	36 ft = _____ yd
3.	12 qt = _____ gal	10 yd = _____ in.
4.	5 gal 2 qt = _____ qt	5 qt 1 pt = _____ pt
5.	7 pt 1 cup = _____ cups	6 gal 3 qt = _____ qt
6.	3 yd 10 in. = _____ in.	7 yd 1 ft = _____ ft
7.	5 ft 11 in. = _____ in.	4 yd 2 ft = _____ ft

Find the perimeter of each figure below.

a

b

c

8.

7 in.

7 in.   7 in.

7 in.

_____ inches

2 ft

3 ft   3 ft

3 ft

_____ feet

7 yd

2 yd   2 yd

7 yd

_____ yards

Find the area of each rectangle below.

9.

9 ft

3 ft

_____ square feet

8 yd

8 yd

_____ square yards

2 in.

6 in.

_____ square inches

Perfect score: 20   My score: _____

77

Write the fraction that tells how much of each figure is colored.

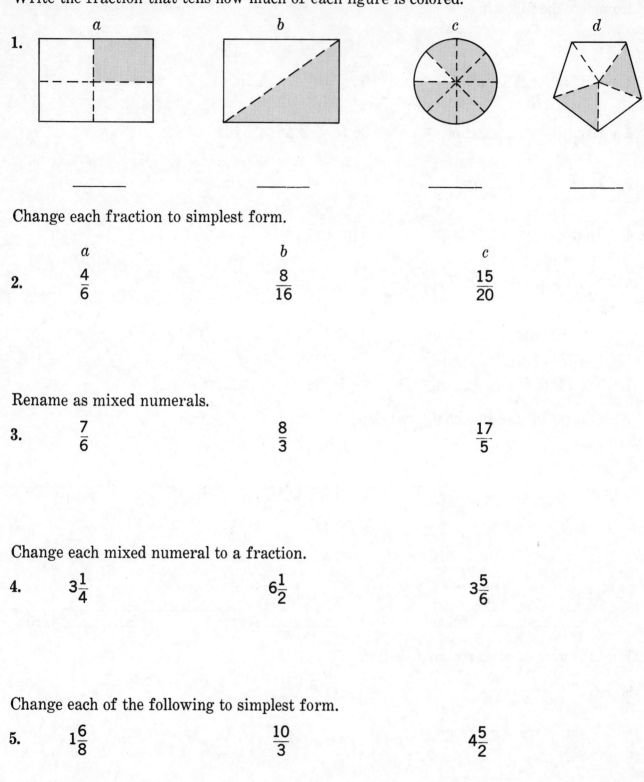

Change each fraction to simplest form.

	a	b	c
2.	$\dfrac{4}{6}$	$\dfrac{8}{16}$	$\dfrac{15}{20}$

Rename as mixed numerals.

| 3. | $\dfrac{7}{6}$ | $\dfrac{8}{3}$ | $\dfrac{17}{5}$ |

Change each mixed numeral to a fraction.

| 4. | $3\dfrac{1}{4}$ | $6\dfrac{1}{2}$ | $3\dfrac{5}{6}$ |

Change each of the following to simplest form.

| 5. | $1\dfrac{6}{8}$ | $\dfrac{10}{3}$ | $4\dfrac{5}{2}$ |

Perfect score: 16   **My score:** _____

78

Lesson 1 Fractions

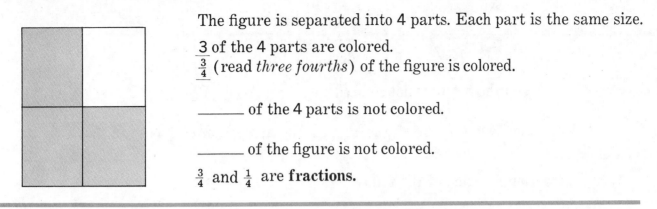

The figure is separated into 4 parts. Each part is the same size.

<u>3</u> of the 4 parts are colored.

$\frac{3}{4}$ (read *three fourths*) of the figure is colored.

_____ of the 4 parts is not colored.

_____ of the figure is not colored.

$\frac{3}{4}$ and $\frac{1}{4}$ are **fractions**.

On the first __ beneath each figure, write the fraction that tells how much of the figure is colored. On the second __, write the fraction that tells how much of the figure is not colored.

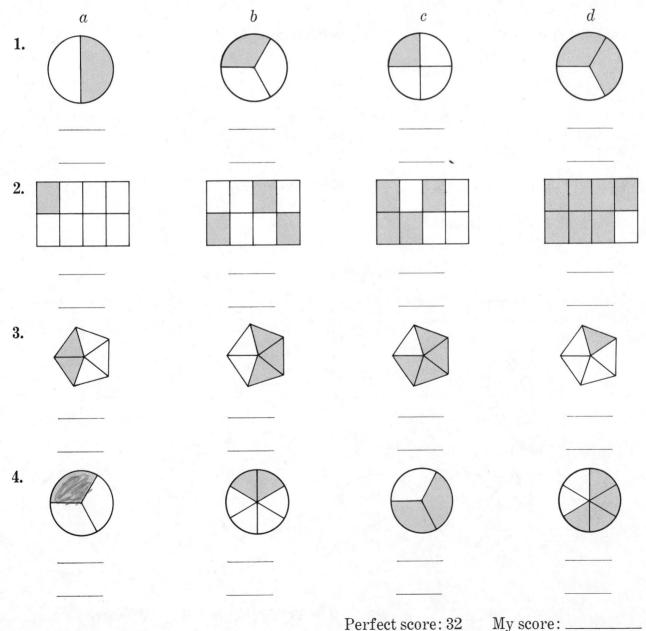

	a	*b*	*c*	*d*
1.				
2.				
3.				
4.				

Perfect score: 32   My score: _____

Lesson 2 Fractions

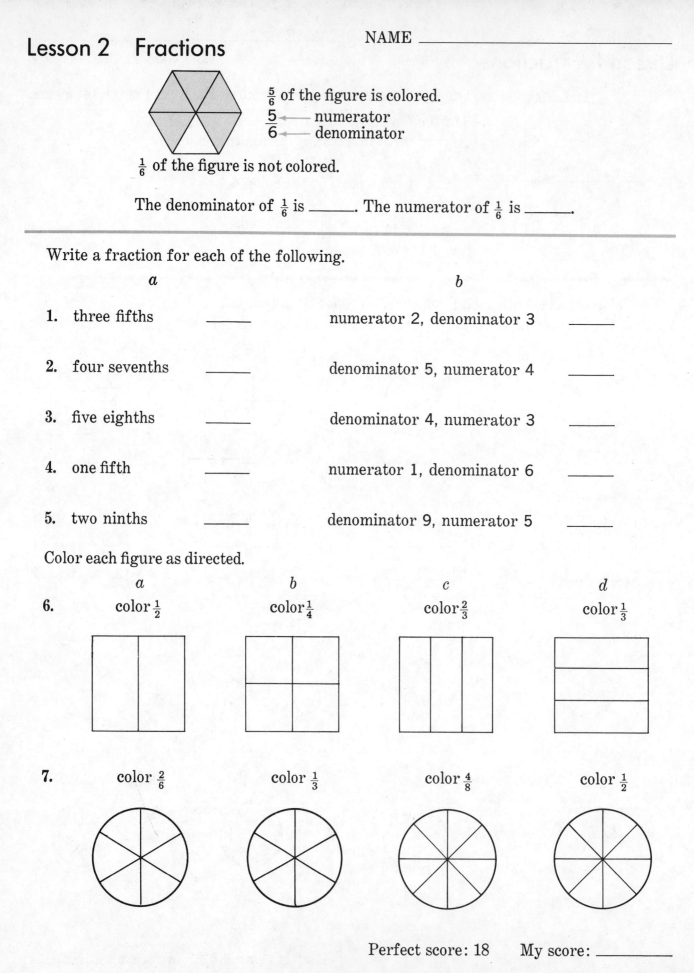

$\frac{5}{6}$ of the figure is colored.

$\underset{6 \longleftarrow \text{ denominator}}{5 \longleftarrow \text{ numerator}}$

$\frac{1}{6}$ of the figure is not colored.

The denominator of $\frac{1}{6}$ is _____. The numerator of $\frac{1}{6}$ is _____.

Write a fraction for each of the following.

	a		b	
1.	three fifths	_____	numerator 2, denominator 3	_____
2.	four sevenths	_____	denominator 5, numerator 4	_____
3.	five eighths	_____	denominator 4, numerator 3	_____
4.	one fifth	_____	numerator 1, denominator 6	_____
5.	two ninths	_____	denominator 9, numerator 5	_____

Color each figure as directed.

               a   *b*   *c*   *d*

6.   color $\frac{1}{2}$ color $\frac{1}{4}$ color $\frac{2}{3}$ color $\frac{1}{3}$

7.   color $\frac{2}{6}$ color $\frac{1}{3}$ color $\frac{4}{8}$ color $\frac{1}{2}$

Perfect score: 18   My score: _____

Lesson 3   Fractions in Simplest Form

A fraction is in simplest form when the only whole number that will divide the numerator and the denominator is 1.

$\dfrac{12}{18} = \dfrac{12 \div 6}{18 \div 6}$ ← Divide both the numerator → $\dfrac{12}{18} = \dfrac{12 \div 2}{18 \div 2}$

$= \dfrac{2}{3}$ and the denominator by the same number.

$= \dfrac{6}{9}$ ← This fraction is not in simplest form so,

$= \dfrac{6 \div 3}{9 \div 3}$ continue dividing the numerator and the

$= \dfrac{2}{3}$ denominator until the fraction is in simplest form.

Change each fraction to simplest form.

	a	*b*	*c*
1.	$\dfrac{4}{6}$	$\dfrac{4}{16}$	$\dfrac{12}{15}$
2.	$\dfrac{12}{32}$	$\dfrac{8}{10}$	$\dfrac{15}{20}$
3.	$\dfrac{14}{16}$	$\dfrac{6}{8}$	$\dfrac{10}{16}$
4.	$\dfrac{6}{10}$	$\dfrac{3}{24}$	$\dfrac{8}{16}$
5.	$\dfrac{14}{21}$	$\dfrac{10}{12}$	$\dfrac{12}{16}$

Perfect score: 15   My score: _____

Fractions in Simplest Form

Change each fraction to simplest form.

	a	*b*	*c*
1.	$\frac{4}{8}$	$\frac{3}{6}$	$\frac{2}{4}$
2.	$\frac{5}{10}$	$\frac{3}{15}$	$\frac{4}{20}$
3.	$\frac{4}{24}$	$\frac{8}{12}$	$\frac{6}{9}$
4.	$\frac{6}{21}$	$\frac{10}{25}$	$\frac{4}{12}$
5.	$\frac{12}{30}$	$\frac{12}{28}$	$\frac{16}{20}$
6.	$\frac{20}{24}$	$\frac{20}{36}$	$\frac{42}{49}$
7.	$\frac{21}{35}$	$\frac{15}{18}$	$\frac{24}{30}$
8.	$\frac{16}{24}$	$\frac{15}{35}$	$\frac{24}{32}$

Perfect score: 24   My score: _____

Lesson 4   Mixed Numerals

$\frac{17}{5}$ means $17 \div 5$ or $5\overline{)17}$.

$$5\overline{)17} \quad \begin{array}{c} 3\frac{2}{5} \\ \hline 17 \\ 15 \\ \hline 2 \end{array} \to 2 \div 5 = \frac{2}{5}$$

$\frac{17}{5} = 3\frac{2}{5}$

$3\frac{2}{5}$ is a **mixed numeral.** It means $3 + \frac{2}{5}$.

Rename as mixed numerals.

	a	*b*	*c*
1.	$\frac{9}{4}$	$\frac{6}{5}$	$\frac{9}{8}$
2.	$\frac{8}{3}$	$\frac{9}{5}$	$\frac{7}{3}$
3.	$\frac{7}{4}$	$\frac{29}{6}$	$\frac{14}{3}$
4.	$\frac{15}{7}$	$\frac{12}{5}$	$\frac{19}{9}$
5.	$\frac{22}{7}$	$\frac{19}{2}$	$\frac{27}{5}$
6.	$\frac{35}{8}$	$\frac{43}{7}$	$\frac{55}{6}$

Perfect score: 18   My score: _____

Lesson 5   Renaming Numbers

Study how to change a mixed numeral to a fraction.

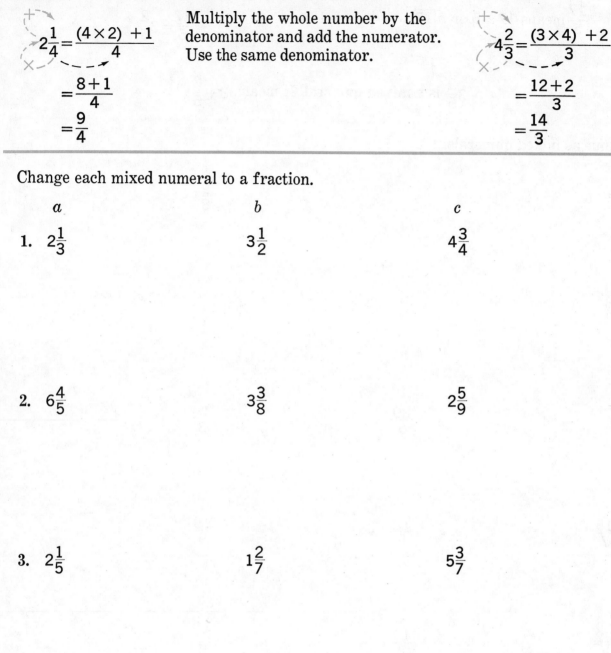

$$2\frac{1}{4} = \frac{(4 \times 2) + 1}{4}$$

$$= \frac{8+1}{4}$$

$$= \frac{9}{4}$$

Multiply the whole number by the denominator and add the numerator. Use the same denominator.

$$4\frac{2}{3} = \frac{(3 \times 4) + 2}{3}$$

$$= \frac{12+2}{3}$$

$$= \frac{14}{3}$$

Change each mixed numeral to a fraction.

	a	*b*	*c*
1.	$2\frac{1}{3}$	$3\frac{1}{2}$	$4\frac{3}{4}$
2.	$6\frac{4}{5}$	$3\frac{3}{8}$	$2\frac{5}{9}$
3.	$2\frac{1}{5}$	$1\frac{2}{7}$	$5\frac{3}{7}$
4.	$6\frac{5}{12}$	$7\frac{3}{10}$	$8\frac{6}{15}$

Perfect score: 12   My score: _____

84

Lesson 6   Mixed Numerals in Simplest Form

A mixed numeral is in simplest form when the fraction is in simplest form and names a number less than 1.

$$5\frac{4}{8} = 5 + \frac{4}{8}$$
$$= 5 + \frac{4 \div 4}{8 \div 4}$$
$$= 5 + \frac{1}{2}$$
$$= 5\frac{1}{2}$$

$$1\frac{18}{8} = 1 + \frac{18}{8}$$
$$= 1 + \frac{18 \div 2}{8 \div 2}$$
$$= 1 + \frac{9}{4}$$
$$= 1 + 2\frac{1}{4}$$
$$= 3\frac{1}{4}$$

$$\frac{9}{4} = 9 \div 4 = 2\frac{1}{4}$$

Change each mixed numeral to simplest form.

	a	*b*	*c*
1.	$3\frac{4}{6}$	$1\frac{4}{8}$	$2\frac{6}{8}$
2.	$4\frac{3}{12}$	$2\frac{6}{16}$	$1\frac{10}{12}$
3.	$1\frac{7}{5}$	$3\frac{9}{6}$	$2\frac{8}{6}$
4.	$1\frac{12}{10}$	$2\frac{15}{10}$	$4\frac{14}{6}$

Perfect score: 12   My score: _____

Lesson 7   Simplest Form

Change each fraction to simplest form.

	a	b	c
1.	$\frac{6}{14}$	$\frac{12}{27}$	$\frac{15}{25}$
2.	$\frac{4}{12}$	$\frac{28}{32}$	$\frac{15}{21}$

Change each of the following to a mixed numeral in simplest form.

3.	$\frac{9}{5}$	$\frac{8}{3}$	$\frac{12}{7}$
4.	$\frac{12}{8}$	$\frac{16}{6}$	$\frac{25}{15}$
5.	$1\frac{8}{10}$	$2\frac{7}{21}$	$3\frac{9}{15}$
6.	$4\frac{12}{14}$	$5\frac{8}{12}$	$2\frac{12}{16}$

Perfect score: 18   My score: _____

CHAPTER 8 TEST

Change each fraction to simplest form.

	a	b	c	d
1.	$\dfrac{4}{8}$	$\dfrac{5}{10}$	$\dfrac{6}{9}$	$\dfrac{3}{6}$
2.	$\dfrac{10}{15}$	$\dfrac{6}{8}$	$\dfrac{12}{18}$	$\dfrac{9}{12}$

Rename as mixed numerals.

3.	$\dfrac{5}{2}$	$\dfrac{7}{5}$	$\dfrac{9}{4}$	$\dfrac{16}{3}$

Change each mixed numeral to a fraction.

4.	$1\dfrac{1}{2}$	$1\dfrac{7}{8}$	$4\dfrac{2}{3}$	$5\dfrac{5}{6}$

Change each of the following to simplest form.

5.	$1\dfrac{8}{10}$	$\dfrac{18}{8}$	$1\dfrac{7}{3}$	$5\dfrac{12}{8}$

Perfect score: 20   My score: _____

PRE-TEST—Multiplication

Write each answer in simplest form.

	a	b	c
1.	$\frac{3}{7} \times \frac{2}{5}$	$\frac{3}{4} \times \frac{7}{8}$	$\frac{4}{5} \times \frac{4}{5}$
2.	$\frac{2}{3} \times \frac{7}{8}$	$\frac{5}{9} \times \frac{3}{5}$	$\frac{9}{10} \times \frac{5}{12}$
3.	$4 \times \frac{2}{3}$	$3 \times \frac{5}{6}$	$\frac{5}{8} \times 10$
4.	$3\frac{1}{5} \times 4$	$2\frac{1}{4} \times 8$	$6 \times 1\frac{5}{6}$
5.	$2\frac{1}{2} \times 2\frac{1}{3}$	$2\frac{1}{4} \times 1\frac{1}{5}$	$1\frac{1}{8} \times 3\frac{1}{3}$

Perfect score: 15   My score: _____

Lesson 1 Multiplication

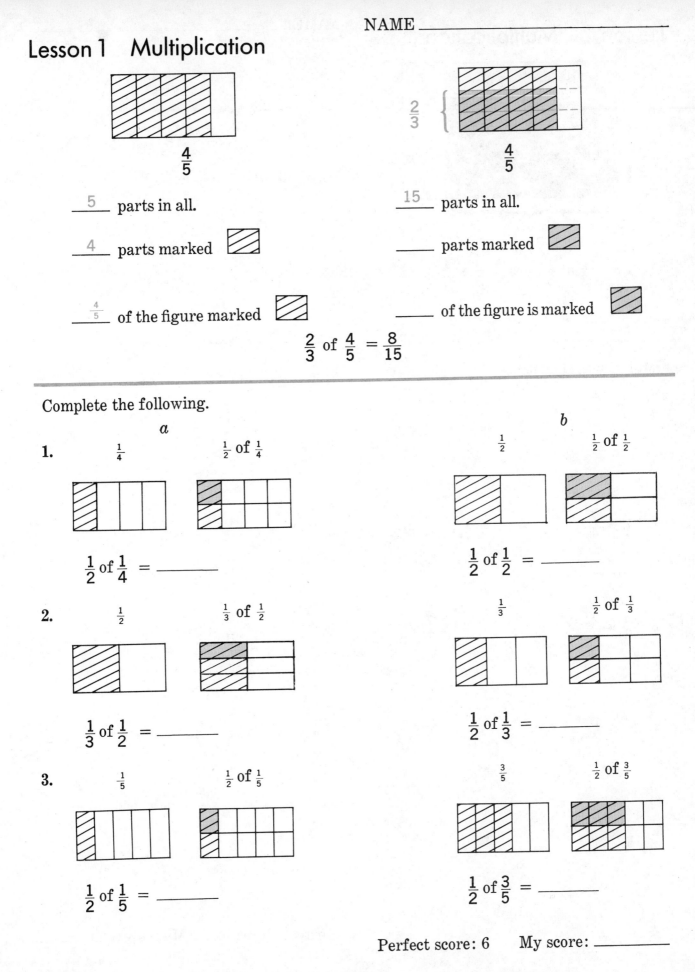

$\dfrac{4}{5}$

__5__ parts in all.

__4__ parts marked

__$\frac{4}{5}$__ of the figure marked

$\dfrac{2}{3}$ {

$\dfrac{4}{5}$

__15__ parts in all.

____ parts marked

____ of the figure is marked

$$\dfrac{2}{3} \text{ of } \dfrac{4}{5} = \dfrac{8}{15}$$

Complete the following.

a   *b*

1. $\dfrac{1}{4}$ $\dfrac{1}{2}$ of $\dfrac{1}{4}$ $\dfrac{1}{2}$ $\dfrac{1}{2}$ of $\dfrac{1}{2}$

$\dfrac{1}{2}$ of $\dfrac{1}{4}$ = _____

$\dfrac{1}{2}$ of $\dfrac{1}{2}$ = _____

2. $\dfrac{1}{2}$ $\dfrac{1}{3}$ of $\dfrac{1}{2}$ $\dfrac{1}{3}$ $\dfrac{1}{2}$ of $\dfrac{1}{3}$

$\dfrac{1}{3}$ of $\dfrac{1}{2}$ = _____

$\dfrac{1}{2}$ of $\dfrac{1}{3}$ = _____

3. $\dfrac{1}{5}$ $\dfrac{1}{2}$ of $\dfrac{1}{5}$ $\dfrac{3}{5}$ $\dfrac{1}{2}$ of $\dfrac{3}{5}$

$\dfrac{1}{2}$ of $\dfrac{1}{5}$ = _____

$\dfrac{1}{2}$ of $\dfrac{3}{5}$ = _____

Perfect score: 6   My score: _____

Lesson 2   Multiplication

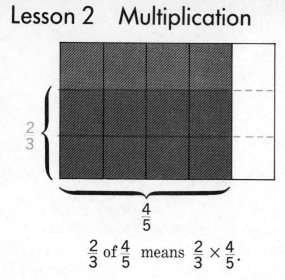

$$\frac{2}{3} \text{ of } \frac{4}{5} \text{ means } \frac{2}{3} \times \frac{4}{5}.$$

Multiply numerators

$$\frac{2}{3} \times \frac{4}{5} = \frac{2 \times 4}{3 \times 5} = \frac{8}{15}$$

Multiply denominators

Multiply as shown.

	a	b	c
1.	$\frac{1}{4} \times \frac{3}{5} = \frac{1 \times 3}{4 \times 5}$ $= \frac{3}{20}$	$\frac{2}{3} \times \frac{1}{5}$	$\frac{1}{6} \times \frac{5}{8}$
2.	$\frac{3}{7} \times \frac{1}{4}$	$\frac{5}{9} \times \frac{1}{2}$	$\frac{6}{7} \times \frac{2}{5}$
3.	$\frac{4}{5} \times \frac{2}{3}$	$\frac{7}{8} \times \frac{1}{6}$	$\frac{1}{5} \times \frac{2}{3}$
4.	$\frac{2}{5} \times \frac{1}{7}$	$\frac{5}{6} \times \frac{1}{2}$	$\frac{2}{3} \times \frac{5}{7}$
5.	$\frac{2}{3} \times \frac{2}{5}$	$\frac{5}{8} \times \frac{3}{4}$	$\frac{2}{5} \times \frac{1}{3}$

Perfect score: 14   My score: _____

90

Lesson 3 Multiplication

$$\frac{4}{5} \times \frac{1}{2} = \frac{4 \times 1}{5 \times 2} \leftarrow \text{Multiply the numerators.} \rightarrow \frac{3}{10} \times \frac{5}{6} = \frac{3 \times 5}{10 \times 6}$$
$$\leftarrow \text{Multiply the denominators.} \rightarrow$$
$$= \frac{4}{10}$$
$$= \frac{15}{60}$$
$$= \frac{2}{5} \leftarrow \begin{array}{c} \text{If necessary, change the} \\ \text{answer to simplest form.} \end{array} \rightarrow = \frac{1}{4}$$

Write each answer in simplest form.

	a	b	c
1.	$\frac{5}{7} \times \frac{1}{4}$	$\frac{3}{5} \times \frac{1}{2}$	$\frac{7}{8} \times \frac{3}{4}$
2.	$\frac{3}{7} \times \frac{2}{5}$	$\frac{1}{4} \times \frac{7}{8}$	$\frac{3}{5} \times \frac{4}{9}$
3.	$\frac{4}{7} \times \frac{3}{8}$	$\frac{9}{10} \times \frac{5}{6}$	$\frac{5}{9} \times \frac{6}{10}$
4.	$\frac{8}{15} \times \frac{5}{12}$	$\frac{5}{12} \times \frac{16}{25}$	$\frac{4}{9} \times \frac{9}{14}$
5.	$\frac{6}{7} \times \frac{2}{3}$	$\frac{7}{8} \times \frac{11}{12}$	$\frac{3}{10} \times \frac{7}{8}$

Perfect score: 15   My score: _____

Problem Solving

Solve. Write each answer in simplest form.

1. Jeff had $\frac{3}{4}$ yard of string. He used $\frac{2}{3}$ of the string to tie a package. How much string did he use?

He used _____ yard.

1.

2. Julia lives $\frac{7}{8}$ mile from work. She has walked $\frac{4}{5}$ of the way to work. How far has she walked?

She has walked _____ mile.

2.

3. Dorothea bought $\frac{1}{2}$ gallon of milk. She drank $\frac{1}{4}$ of it. How much milk did she drink?

She drank _____ gallon.

3.

4. Stewart bought $\frac{3}{4}$ pound of cheese. He ate $\frac{1}{3}$ of it. How much cheese did he eat?

He ate _____ pound.

4.

5. Five sixths of a room is now painted. Carlos did $\frac{2}{5}$ of the painting. How much of the room did he paint?

He painted _____ of the room.

5.

6. The lawn is $\frac{1}{2}$ mowed. Melinda did $\frac{2}{3}$ of the mowing. How much of the lawn did she mow?

She mowed _____ of the lawn.

6.

7. A lawn mower uses $\frac{3}{4}$ gallon of fuel each hour. How much fuel will it use in $\frac{1}{2}$ hour?

It will use _____ gallon.

7.

Perfect score: 7   My score: _____

92

Lesson 4 Multiplication

$$4 \times \frac{2}{5} = \frac{4}{1} \times \frac{2}{5}$$

Name the whole number as a fraction.

$$\frac{5}{8} \times 6 = \frac{5}{8} \times \frac{6}{1}$$

$$= \frac{4 \times 2}{1 \times 5}$$

Multiply the fractions.

$$= \frac{5 \times 6}{8 \times 1}$$

$$= \frac{8}{5}$$

$$= \frac{30}{8}$$

$$1\frac{3}{5}$$
$$5\overline{)8}$$

$$3\frac{3}{4}$$
$$8\overline{)30}$$

$$= 1\frac{3}{5}$$

Change the answer to simplest form.

$$= 3\frac{3}{4}$$

Write each answer in simplest form.

	a	b	c
1.	$5 \times \frac{3}{7}$	$9 \times \frac{7}{8}$	$7 \times \frac{5}{6}$
2.	$\frac{2}{3} \times 5$	$\frac{7}{8} \times 9$	$\frac{4}{5} \times 12$
3.	$8 \times \frac{3}{4}$	$9 \times \frac{5}{6}$	$4 \times \frac{4}{5}$
4.	$\frac{7}{8} \times 12$	$\frac{3}{5} \times 10$	$\frac{5}{6} \times 14$

Perfect score: 12   My score: _____

Problem Solving

Solve. Write each answer in simplest form.

1. A boy weighs 60 pounds on Earth. He would weigh only $\frac{1}{6}$ of that on the moon. How much would he weigh on the moon?

He would weigh _____ pounds.

2. A woman weighs 120 pounds on Earth. How much would she weigh on the moon?

She would weigh _____ pounds.

3. A dog weighs 20 pounds on Earth. It would weigh only $\frac{2}{5}$ of that on Mars. How much would the dog weigh on Mars?

It would weigh _____ pounds.

4. How much would the boy in problem **1** weigh on Mars?

He would weigh _____ pounds.

5. How much would the woman in problem **2** weigh on Mars?

She would weigh _____ pounds.

6. A rock weighs 10 pounds on Earth. It would weigh only $\frac{7}{8}$ of that on Venus. How much would it weigh on Venus?

It would weigh _____ pounds.

7. How much would the dog in problem **3** weigh on Venus?

It would weigh _____ pounds.

1.	
2.	
3.	
4.	
5.	
6.	
7.	

Perfect score: 7   My score: _____

Lesson 5 Multiplication

$$2\frac{1}{6} \times 8 = \frac{13}{6} \times \frac{8}{1}$$

Change the mixed numeral to a fraction.
Name the whole number as a fraction.

$$= \frac{13 \times 8}{6 \times 1}$$

Multiply.

$$= \frac{104}{6}$$

$$= 17\frac{1}{3}$$

Change the answer
to simplest form.

Write each answer in simplest form.

a	b	c
1. $4\frac{1}{2} \times 5$	$1\frac{3}{4} \times 7$	$3 \times 2\frac{1}{8}$
2. $2\frac{2}{3} \times 6$	$1\frac{7}{8} \times 6$	$4 \times 2\frac{3}{8}$
3. $2\frac{4}{5} \times 7$	$10 \times 2\frac{4}{15}$	$8\frac{1}{7} \times 4$
4. $8 \times 2\frac{5}{6}$	$3\frac{2}{7} \times 14$	$3\frac{1}{3} \times 7$

Perfect score: 12   My score: _____

Problem Solving

Solve. Write each answer in simplest form.

1. Some square tiles measure $3\frac{1}{2}$ inches on each side. Seven tiles are placed in a row. How long is the row of tiles?

The row would be _____ inches long.

2. Suppose that 10 tiles like those in problem **1** were placed in a row. How long would that row of tiles be?

It would be _____ inches long.

3. There are 5 boxes and each one weighs $1\frac{3}{4}$ pounds. How many pounds do all the boxes weigh?

All the boxes weigh _____ pounds.

4. Each board is $1\frac{5}{8}$ inches thick. Six boards are stacked on top of each other. How high is the stack?

The stack of boards is _____ inches high.

5. Suppose it takes $2\frac{5}{6}$ hours to make an orbit around the moon. How long would it take to make 9 orbits?

It would take _____ hours.

6. There are a dozen boxes of nails in each carton. Each box of nails weighs $2\frac{1}{2}$ pounds. How much would a carton of nails weigh?

One carton would weigh _____ pounds.

7. In problem **6**, suppose there are only 6 boxes left in the carton. How much would that carton weigh?

It would weigh _____ pounds.

8. Each straight piece of road-racing track is $5\frac{3}{8}$ inches long. What would the total length of track be if Jill lays 10 pieces of straight track end-to-end?

The total length would be _____ inches.

1.

2.

3.

4.

5.

6.

7.

8.

Perfect score: 8   My score: _____

Lesson 6   Multiplication

$$1\frac{1}{2} \times 2\frac{1}{4} = \frac{3}{2} \times \frac{9}{4}$$ Change both mixed numerals to fractions.

$$= \frac{3 \times 9}{2 \times 4}$$ Multiply.

$$= \frac{27}{8}$$

$$= 3\frac{3}{8}$$ Change to simplest form.

Write each answer in simplest form.

	a	b	c
1.	$3\frac{1}{8} \times 1\frac{2}{3}$	$1\frac{1}{6} \times 2\frac{1}{2}$	$1\frac{4}{5} \times 1\frac{3}{4}$
2.	$2\frac{2}{3} \times 4\frac{1}{5}$	$2\frac{1}{2} \times 1\frac{1}{7}$	$1\frac{3}{5} \times 1\frac{1}{6}$
3.	$1\frac{3}{5} \times 3\frac{3}{4}$	$2\frac{1}{4} \times 3\frac{1}{3}$	$4\frac{1}{2} \times 2\frac{2}{3}$
4.	$2\frac{2}{5} \times 2\frac{1}{4}$	$1\frac{3}{8} \times 1\frac{3}{7}$	$2\frac{4}{5} \times 2\frac{6}{7}$

Perfect score: 12   My score: _____

Problem Solving

Solve. Write each answer in simplest form.

1. A rectangle is $4\frac{1}{2}$ feet long and $1\frac{3}{4}$ feet wide. Find the area of the rectangle.

1.

The area is _____ square feet.

2. A rectangular picture is $1\frac{3}{4}$ inches long and $3\frac{1}{2}$ inches wide. Find the area of the picture.

2.

The area is _____ square inches.

3. A rectangular window is $2\frac{1}{2}$ feet long and $4\frac{1}{2}$ feet wide. Find the area of the window.

3.

The area is _____ square feet.

4. Each side of a square floor is $10\frac{1}{2}$ feet long. Find the area of that floor.

4.

The area is _____ square feet.

5. A boat was traveling $12\frac{1}{2}$ miles each hour. At that rate, how many miles would it travel in $1\frac{1}{2}$ hours?

5.

It would travel _____ miles.

6. How many miles would the boat in problem 5 travel in 4 hours?

6.

It would travel _____ miles.

7. How many miles would the boat in problem 5 travel in $5\frac{1}{4}$ hours?

7.

It would travel _____ miles.

Perfect score: 7   My score: _____

Lesson 7   Multiplication

Write each answer in simplest form.

	a	b	c	d
1.	$\frac{3}{4} \times \frac{1}{5}$	$\frac{2}{7} \times \frac{3}{5}$	$\frac{2}{3} \times \frac{1}{5}$	$\frac{5}{12} \times \frac{7}{8}$
2.	$\frac{6}{7} \times \frac{1}{3}$	$\frac{4}{7} \times \frac{5}{6}$	$\frac{3}{8} \times \frac{2}{9}$	$\frac{3}{4} \times \frac{5}{12}$
3.	$6 \times \frac{2}{5}$	$\frac{2}{7} \times 4$	$8 \times \frac{3}{4}$	$\frac{3}{8} \times 6$
4.	$6\frac{2}{5} \times 5$	$6\frac{7}{8} \times 16$	$4 \times 5\frac{5}{6}$	$8 \times 2\frac{1}{12}$
5.	$3\frac{1}{8} \times 3\frac{1}{5}$	$4\frac{2}{3} \times 1\frac{4}{5}$	$2\frac{1}{2} \times 4\frac{2}{3}$	$1\frac{3}{5} \times 1\frac{1}{4}$

Perfect score: 20   My score: _____

Problem Solving

Solve. Write each answer in simplest form.

1. Zoe spent $\frac{2}{3}$ hour doing homework. She spent $\frac{3}{4}$ of this time reading. How long did she spend reading?

She spent _____ hour reading.

2. A rectangular picture is $8\frac{1}{2}$ inches long and 10 inches wide. Find the area of the picture.

The area is _____ square inches.

3. In one hour a machine can produce $\frac{9}{10}$ pound of silver. Suppose the machine breaks down after $\frac{1}{3}$ hour. How many pounds of silver are processed?

_____ pound of silver is processed.

4. A certain book is $\frac{7}{8}$ inch thick. Ten of these books are placed on top of each other. How high is the stack?

The stack of books will be _____ inches high.

5. A large box of Lotsa-clean detergent weighs $6\frac{3}{4}$ pounds. There are 12 of these boxes in a carton. How much would a carton weigh?

A carton would weigh _____ pounds.

6. There are $4\frac{1}{2}$ pounds of dog food in each bag. How many pounds of dog food would be in 3 bags?

There would be _____ pounds in 3 bags.

7. Basil gained 3 pounds in six months. Floyd gained $3\frac{1}{9}$ times as many pounds as Basil. How many pounds did Floyd gain?

Floyd gained _____ pounds.

1.	
2.	
3.	
4.	
5.	
6.	
7.	

Perfect score: 7   My score: _____

100

CHAPTER 9 TEST

Write each answer in simplest form.

	a	b	c

1. $\dfrac{7}{8} \times \dfrac{5}{6}$ $\dfrac{4}{5} \times \dfrac{3}{7}$ $\dfrac{2}{3} \times \dfrac{1}{5}$

2. $\dfrac{2}{3} \times \dfrac{5}{6}$ $\dfrac{8}{9} \times \dfrac{3}{8}$ $\dfrac{2}{5} \times \dfrac{15}{16}$

3. $8 \times \dfrac{3}{5}$ $9 \times \dfrac{5}{6}$ $\dfrac{3}{4} \times 20$

4. $2\dfrac{2}{5} \times 4$ $4\dfrac{1}{4} \times 6$ $3 \times 1\dfrac{2}{9}$

5. $\dfrac{2}{3} \times 1\dfrac{4}{5}$ $7\dfrac{1}{2} \times \dfrac{4}{5}$ $6\dfrac{1}{4} \times \dfrac{2}{5}$

6. $1\dfrac{3}{5} \times 1\dfrac{1}{3}$ $2\dfrac{1}{2} \times 3\dfrac{1}{3}$ $2\dfrac{1}{6} \times 1\dfrac{1}{8}$

Perfect score: 18   My score: _____

Write each answer in simplest form.

	a	b	c	d

1.
$\begin{array}{r} \frac{1}{6} \\ +\frac{1}{6} \\ \hline \end{array}$
$\qquad$
$\begin{array}{r} \frac{3}{8} \\ +\frac{1}{8} \\ \hline \end{array}$
$\qquad$
$\begin{array}{r} \frac{5}{9} \\ +\frac{2}{9} \\ \hline \end{array}$
$\qquad$
$\begin{array}{r} \frac{7}{12} \\ +\frac{5}{12} \\ \hline \end{array}$

2.
$\begin{array}{r} \frac{5}{6} \\ +\frac{1}{3} \\ \hline \end{array}$
$\qquad$
$\begin{array}{r} \frac{7}{8} \\ +\frac{1}{2} \\ \hline \end{array}$
$\qquad$
$\begin{array}{r} \frac{7}{10} \\ +\frac{2}{5} \\ \hline \end{array}$
$\qquad$
$\begin{array}{r} \frac{3}{5} \\ +\frac{1}{4} \\ \hline \end{array}$

3.
$\begin{array}{r} 7\frac{1}{2} \\ +3\frac{1}{4} \\ \hline \end{array}$
$\qquad$
$\begin{array}{r} 6\frac{7}{10} \\ +1\frac{1}{5} \\ \hline \end{array}$
$\qquad$
$\begin{array}{r} 5\frac{1}{3} \\ +\frac{3}{4} \\ \hline \end{array}$
$\qquad$
$\begin{array}{r} 4\frac{1}{3} \\ +2\frac{1}{2} \\ \hline \end{array}$

4.
$\begin{array}{r} 1\frac{5}{8} \\ +4\frac{1}{6} \\ \hline \end{array}$
$\qquad$
$\begin{array}{r} 5\frac{3}{4} \\ +\frac{1}{5} \\ \hline \end{array}$
$\qquad$
$\begin{array}{r} \frac{7}{12} \\ +\frac{5}{6} \\ \hline \end{array}$
$\qquad$
$\begin{array}{r} \frac{1}{12} \\ +6\frac{3}{4} \\ \hline \end{array}$

5.
$\begin{array}{r} \frac{2}{3} \\ +\frac{3}{4} \\ \hline \end{array}$
$\qquad$
$\begin{array}{r} 9\frac{3}{8} \\ +\frac{1}{4} \\ \hline \end{array}$
$\qquad$
$\begin{array}{r} 3\frac{4}{5} \\ +1\frac{3}{10} \\ \hline \end{array}$
$\qquad$
$\begin{array}{r} 4\frac{2}{3} \\ +5\frac{5}{6} \\ \hline \end{array}$

10

Perfect score: 20   My score: _____

Lesson 1   Addition

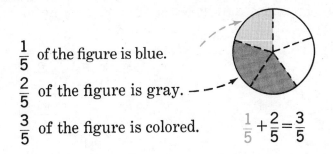

$\dfrac{1}{5}$ of the figure is blue.

$\dfrac{2}{5}$ of the figure is gray. ---

$\dfrac{3}{5}$ of the figure is colored. $\dfrac{1}{5} + \dfrac{2}{5} = \dfrac{3}{5}$

Complete the following.

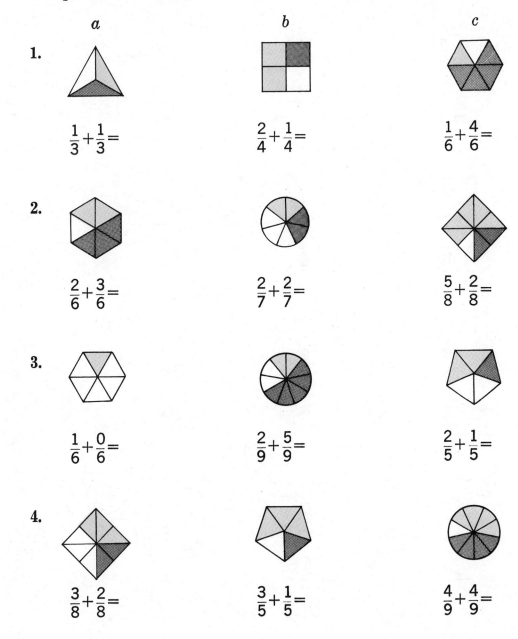

	a	*b*	*c*
1.	$\dfrac{1}{3} + \dfrac{1}{3} =$	$\dfrac{2}{4} + \dfrac{1}{4} =$	$\dfrac{1}{6} + \dfrac{4}{6} =$
2.	$\dfrac{2}{6} + \dfrac{3}{6} =$	$\dfrac{2}{7} + \dfrac{2}{7} =$	$\dfrac{5}{8} + \dfrac{2}{8} =$
3.	$\dfrac{1}{6} + \dfrac{0}{6} =$	$\dfrac{2}{9} + \dfrac{5}{9} =$	$\dfrac{2}{5} + \dfrac{1}{5} =$
4.	$\dfrac{3}{8} + \dfrac{2}{8} =$	$\dfrac{3}{5} + \dfrac{1}{5} =$	$\dfrac{4}{9} + \dfrac{4}{9} =$

Perfect score: 12   My score: _____

103

Lesson 2   Addition

NAME _____

Study how to add two fractions that have the same denominator.

Add the numerators.

$$\frac{3}{8}+\frac{2}{8}=\frac{3+2}{8}=\frac{5}{8}$$

Use the same denominator.

Add the numerators.

$$\begin{array}{r}\frac{3}{8}\\+\frac{2}{8}\\\hline\frac{5}{8}\end{array}$$

Use the same denominator.

Add.

	a	b	c	d	e
1.	$\dfrac{1}{3}$ $+\dfrac{1}{3}$	$\dfrac{2}{7}$ $+\dfrac{4}{7}$	$\dfrac{5}{8}$ $+\dfrac{2}{8}$	$\dfrac{1}{4}$ $+\dfrac{2}{4}$	$\dfrac{2}{5}$ $+\dfrac{2}{5}$
2.	$\dfrac{4}{9}$ $+\dfrac{3}{9}$	$\dfrac{4}{8}$ $+\dfrac{1}{8}$	$\dfrac{1}{6}$ $+\dfrac{4}{6}$	$\dfrac{3}{7}$ $+\dfrac{3}{7}$	$\dfrac{2}{10}$ $+\dfrac{5}{10}$
3.	$\dfrac{2}{5}$ $+\dfrac{1}{5}$	$\dfrac{3}{6}$ $+\dfrac{2}{6}$	$\dfrac{2}{8}$ $+\dfrac{1}{8}$	$\dfrac{2}{7}$ $+\dfrac{2}{7}$	$\dfrac{2}{9}$ $+\dfrac{2}{9}$
4.	$\dfrac{1}{9}$ $+\dfrac{4}{9}$	$\dfrac{1}{7}$ $+\dfrac{4}{7}$	$\dfrac{6}{8}$ $+\dfrac{1}{8}$	$\dfrac{1}{5}$ $+\dfrac{1}{5}$	$\dfrac{3}{7}$ $+\dfrac{1}{7}$

Perfect score: 20   My score: _____

104

Lesson 3 Addition

$$\frac{7}{10}$$
$$+\frac{9}{10}$$
$$\frac{16}{10}=1\frac{3}{5}$$

Add.

Change to simplest form.

$$\frac{1}{12}$$
$$+\frac{11}{12}$$
$$\frac{12}{12}=1$$

Add. Write each answer in simplest form.

	a	*b*	*c*	*d*
1.	$\frac{2}{3}$ $+\frac{2}{3}$	$\frac{4}{5}$ $+\frac{3}{5}$	$\frac{2}{9}$ $+\frac{1}{9}$	$\frac{1}{4}$ $+\frac{1}{4}$
2.	$\frac{1}{8}$ $+\frac{5}{8}$	$\frac{3}{10}$ $+\frac{9}{10}$	$\frac{3}{4}$ $+\frac{3}{4}$	$\frac{7}{12}$ $+\frac{11}{12}$
3.	$\frac{1}{2}$ $+\frac{1}{2}$	$\frac{6}{7}$ $+\frac{5}{7}$	$\frac{7}{8}$ $+\frac{7}{8}$	$\frac{5}{6}$ $+\frac{1}{6}$
4.	$\frac{3}{5}$ $+\frac{3}{5}$	$\frac{5}{12}$ $+\frac{7}{12}$	$\frac{8}{9}$ $+\frac{5}{9}$	$\frac{7}{10}$ $+\frac{9}{10}$

Perfect score: 16   My score: _____

Lesson 4   Addition

$$4\frac{5}{8}$$

$$+2\frac{1}{8}$$

$$6\frac{6}{8}=6\frac{3}{4}$$

Add the fractions.

Add the whole numbers.

Change to simplest form.

$$6\frac{7}{10}$$

$$+2\frac{9}{10}$$

$$8\frac{16}{10}=9\frac{3}{5}$$

Add. Write each answer in simplest form.

a	b	c	d

1. $1\frac{2}{5}$ $4\frac{1}{6}$ $3\frac{1}{10}$ $19\frac{3}{8}$

  $+2\frac{1}{5}$ $+2\frac{1}{6}$ $+2\frac{3}{10}$ $+7\frac{1}{8}$

2. $5\frac{3}{4}$ $6\frac{2}{3}$ $2\frac{9}{10}$ $26\frac{4}{5}$

  $+1\frac{3}{4}$ $+1\frac{1}{3}$ $+1\frac{7}{10}$ $+13\frac{3}{5}$

3. $4\frac{1}{2}$ $3\frac{5}{6}$ $8\frac{7}{12}$ $36\frac{7}{8}$

  $+2\frac{1}{2}$ $+4\frac{5}{6}$ $+4\frac{11}{12}$ $+27\frac{5}{8}$

4. $7\frac{2}{3}$ $9\frac{2}{5}$ $11\frac{3}{10}$ $58\frac{7}{9}$

  $+6\frac{2}{3}$ $+4\frac{4}{5}$ $+6\frac{7}{10}$ $+31\frac{5}{9}$

Perfect score: 16   My score: _____

106

Lesson 5   Renaming Fractions

By separating the figure in different ways, you can write different fractions to tell how much is orange.

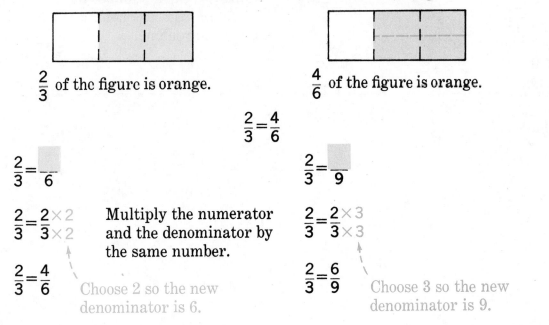

$\frac{2}{3}$ of the figure is orange.

$\frac{4}{6}$ of the figure is orange.

$$\frac{2}{3} = \frac{4}{6}$$

$\frac{2}{3} = \frac{}{6}$

$\frac{2}{3} = \frac{}{9}$

$\frac{2}{3} = \frac{2 \times 2}{3 \times 2}$

Multiply the numerator and the denominator by the same number.

$\frac{2}{3} = \frac{2 \times 3}{3 \times 3}$

$\frac{2}{3} = \frac{4}{6}$

Choose 2 so the new denominator is 6.

$\frac{2}{3} = \frac{6}{9}$

Choose 3 so the new denominator is 9.

Rename.

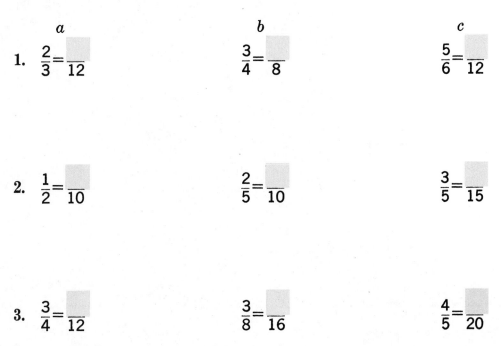

     a   *b*   *c*

1. $\frac{2}{3} = \frac{}{12}$ $\frac{3}{4} = \frac{}{8}$ $\frac{5}{6} = \frac{}{12}$

2. $\frac{1}{2} = \frac{}{10}$ $\frac{2}{5} = \frac{}{10}$ $\frac{3}{5} = \frac{}{15}$

3. $\frac{3}{4} = \frac{}{12}$ $\frac{3}{8} = \frac{}{16}$ $\frac{4}{5} = \frac{}{20}$

Perfect score: 9   My score: _____

Renaming Numbers

$$\frac{7}{8}=\frac{\boxed{}}{32}$$

$$\frac{7}{8}=\frac{7\times4}{8\times4}$$

$$\frac{7}{8}=\frac{28}{32}$$

$$7=\frac{\boxed{}}{3}$$

$$7=\frac{7\times3}{1\times3}$$

$$7=\frac{21}{3}$$

Name the whole number as
a fraction whose denominator
is 1. Then rename.

Rename.

	a	*b*	*c*
1.	$\frac{1}{2}=\frac{\boxed{}}{4}$	$\frac{1}{3}=\frac{\boxed{}}{9}$	$3=\frac{\boxed{}}{12}$
2.	$6=\frac{\boxed{}}{}$	$4\,\frac{\boxed{}}{}$	$7=\frac{\boxed{}}{5}$
3.			$4=\frac{\boxed{}}{3}$
4.	$\frac{1}{3}=\frac{\boxed{}}{6}$	$\frac{1}{2}=\frac{\boxed{}}{8}$	$6=\frac{\boxed{}}{6}$

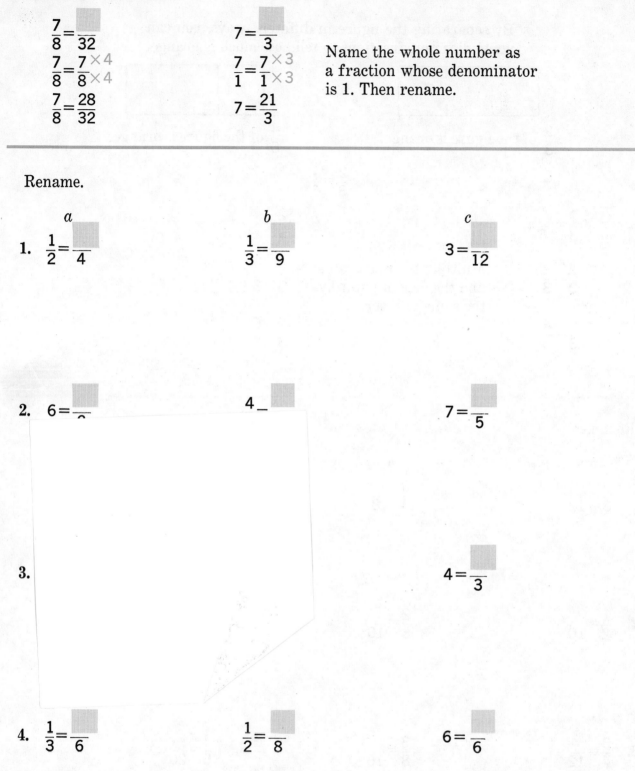

Perfect score: 12   My score: _____

108

Lesson 6   Addition

When adding fractions that have different denominators, rename the fractions so they have the same denominator.

$$\frac{1}{3} \quad \times\frac{2}{2} \quad \frac{2}{6}$$
$$+\frac{1}{2} \quad \times\frac{3}{3} \quad +\frac{3}{6}$$
$$\frac{5}{6}$$

The denominators are 2 and 3. Since $2 \times 3 = 6$, rename each fraction with a denominator of 6.

Then add the fractions.

$$\frac{1}{2} \quad \times\frac{3}{3} \quad \frac{3}{6}$$
$$+\frac{2}{3} \quad \times\frac{2}{2} \quad +\frac{4}{6}$$
$$\frac{7}{6} = 1\frac{1}{6}$$

Change $\frac{7}{6}$ to a mixed numeral in simplest form.

Write each answer in simplest form.

	a	b	c	d
1.	$\frac{2}{5}$ $+\frac{1}{2}$	$\frac{1}{4}$ $+\frac{2}{3}$	$\frac{2}{5}$ $+\frac{1}{3}$	$\frac{1}{2}$ $+\frac{1}{5}$
2.	$\frac{5}{6}$ $+\frac{3}{5}$	$\frac{2}{3}$ $+\frac{1}{5}$	$\frac{1}{3}$ $+\frac{3}{10}$	$\frac{5}{8}$ $+\frac{2}{3}$
3.	$\frac{3}{4}$ $+\frac{1}{3}$	$\frac{2}{3}$ $+\frac{4}{5}$	$\frac{2}{3}$ $+\frac{3}{4}$	$\frac{7}{8}$ $+\frac{1}{3}$

Perfect score: 12   My score: _____

Addition

$$\frac{2}{5} \quad \boxed{\times\frac{2}{2}} \quad \frac{4}{10}$$
$$+\frac{3}{10} \longrightarrow +\frac{3}{10}$$
$$\frac{7}{10}$$

The denominators are 5 and 10. Since $2 \times 5 = 10$, rename only $\frac{2}{5}$ with a denominator of 10.

Then add the fractions.

$$\frac{7}{10} \longrightarrow \frac{7}{10}$$
$$+\frac{2}{5} \quad \boxed{\times\frac{2}{2}} \quad +\frac{4}{10}$$
$$\frac{11}{10} = 1\frac{1}{10}$$

Change $\frac{11}{10}$ to simplest form.

Write each answer in simplest form.

	a	*b*	*c*	*d*
1.	$\frac{3}{4}$	$\frac{2}{3}$	$\frac{1}{2}$	$\frac{5}{12}$
	$+\frac{1}{8}$	$+\frac{5}{6}$	$+\frac{3}{10}$	$+\frac{2}{3}$
2.	$\frac{5}{16}$	$\frac{1}{6}$	$\frac{5}{8}$	$\frac{9}{10}$
	$+\frac{3}{8}$	$+\frac{1}{2}$	$+\frac{1}{4}$	$+\frac{3}{5}$
3.	$\frac{3}{4}$	$\frac{5}{12}$	$\frac{5}{6}$	$\frac{1}{2}$
	$+\frac{9}{16}$	$+\frac{1}{4}$	$+\frac{1}{3}$	$+\frac{7}{8}$

Perfect score: 12   My score: _____

110

Lesson 7   Addition

$\dfrac{1}{6}$ $\times\dfrac{4}{4}$ $\dfrac{4}{24}$ The denominators are 6 and 8. $\dfrac{5}{6}$ $\times\dfrac{4}{4}$ $\dfrac{20}{24}$

$+\dfrac{5}{8}$ $\times\dfrac{3}{3}$ $+\dfrac{15}{24}$ Since $4\times6=24$ and $3\times8=24$, $+\dfrac{3}{8}$ $\times\dfrac{3}{3}$ $+\dfrac{9}{24}$

$\dfrac{19}{24}$ rename each fraction with a denominator of 24. $\dfrac{29}{24}=1\dfrac{5}{24}$ Change $\dfrac{29}{24}$ to simplest form.

Then add the fractions.

Write each answer in simplest form.

	a	*b*	*c*	*d*
1.	$\dfrac{1}{9}$ $+\dfrac{1}{6}$	$\dfrac{1}{6}$ $+\dfrac{1}{4}$	$\dfrac{5}{6}$ $+\dfrac{1}{8}$	$\dfrac{1}{10}$ $+\dfrac{1}{12}$
2.	$\dfrac{1}{6}$ $+\dfrac{3}{8}$	$\dfrac{3}{4}$ $+\dfrac{1}{6}$	$\dfrac{5}{6}$ $+\dfrac{5}{8}$	$\dfrac{3}{10}$ $+\dfrac{3}{8}$
3.	$\dfrac{3}{10}$ $+\dfrac{5}{12}$	$\dfrac{5}{6}$ $+\dfrac{4}{9}$	$\dfrac{3}{10}$ $+\dfrac{1}{4}$	$\dfrac{5}{6}$ $+\dfrac{3}{10}$
4.	$\dfrac{7}{10}$ $+\dfrac{5}{6}$	$\dfrac{11}{12}$ $+\dfrac{7}{8}$	$\dfrac{9}{10}$ $+\dfrac{7}{8}$	$\dfrac{1}{4}$ $+\dfrac{5}{6}$

Perfect score: 16   My score: _____

Problem Solving

Solve. Write each answer in simplest form.

1. To make green paint, Andrea mixed $\frac{7}{8}$ quart of yellow paint and $\frac{1}{2}$ quart of blue paint. How much green paint did she make?

She made _____ quarts of green paint.

2. Sean painted $\frac{1}{3}$ of a fence. Sandra painted $\frac{1}{4}$ of the fence. How much of the fence did they paint?

They painted _____ of the fence.

3. Maureen bought $\frac{3}{4}$ pound of cheese. Chang bought $\frac{1}{2}$ pound of cheese. How much cheese did they buy?

They bought _____ pounds of cheese.

4. A recipe calls for $\frac{2}{3}$ cup of milk and $\frac{3}{4}$ cup of water. How much milk and water are to be used?

_____ cups of milk and water are to be used.

5. A board $\frac{1}{2}$ inch thick is glued to a board $\frac{3}{8}$ inch thick. What is the combined thickness?

The combined thickness is _____ inch.

6. A book $\frac{3}{4}$ inch thick is placed on a book $\frac{13}{16}$ inch thick. What is the combined thickness of the books?

The combined thickness is _____ inches.

7. Yesterday $\frac{3}{10}$ inch of rain fell. Today $\frac{3}{4}$ inch of rain fell. How much rain fell during the two days?

_____ inches of rain fell during the two days.

1.	
2.	3.
4.	5.
6.	7.

Perfect score: 7   My score: _____

112

Lesson 8   Addition

Rename the fractions so they
have the same denominator.

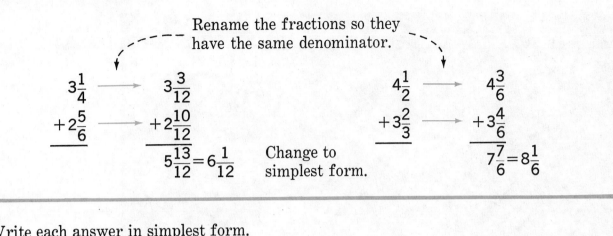

$3\frac{1}{4} \longrightarrow 3\frac{3}{12}$

$+2\frac{5}{6} \longrightarrow +2\frac{10}{12}$

$5\frac{13}{12} = 6\frac{1}{12}$ Change to simplest form.

$4\frac{1}{2} \longrightarrow 4\frac{3}{6}$

$+3\frac{2}{3} \longrightarrow +3\frac{4}{6}$

$7\frac{7}{6} = 8\frac{1}{6}$

Write each answer in simplest form.

	a	*b*	*c*	*d*
1.	$3\frac{5}{6}$ $+4\frac{5}{8}$	$5\frac{2}{3}$ $+1\frac{5}{6}$	$6\frac{5}{6}$ $+3\frac{1}{4}$	$\frac{1}{2}$ $+2\frac{3}{4}$
2.	$1\frac{5}{6}$ $+4\frac{1}{3}$	$5\frac{1}{2}$ $+2\frac{3}{4}$	$3\frac{2}{3}$ $+\ \frac{3}{4}$	$2\frac{3}{5}$ $+1\frac{1}{2}$
3.	$4\frac{3}{8}$ $+6\frac{1}{4}$	$5\frac{1}{3}$ $+\ \frac{2}{5}$	$4\frac{2}{5}$ $+2\frac{3}{10}$	$2\frac{1}{8}$ $+5\frac{3}{4}$
4.	$3\frac{1}{2}$ $+3\frac{1}{2}$	$1\frac{3}{8}$ $+2\frac{1}{2}$	$9\frac{3}{4}$ $+6\frac{1}{2}$	$12\frac{2}{3}$ $+1\frac{5}{6}$

Perfect score: 16   My score: _____

Problem Solving

Solve each problem.

1. Jennifer spent $1\frac{1}{2}$ hours working on Ms. Thomkin's car on Monday. She spent $2\frac{3}{4}$ more hours on Tuesday to finish the tune-up. How many hours in all did she work on Ms. Thomkin's car?

She worked _____ hours in all.

1.

2. Myrna worked $7\frac{1}{4}$ hours Monday. She worked $9\frac{3}{4}$ hours Tuesday. How many hours did she work in all on Monday and Tuesday?

She worked _____ hours in all on Monday and Tuesday.

2.

3. The auto repair shop is $1\frac{3}{10}$ miles from the bank. The bank is $3\frac{3}{5}$ miles from Melinda's home. After she left her car at the shop, Melinda walked to the bank. Then she walked home. How far did Melinda walk in all?

Melinda walked _____ miles.

3.

4. It took $2\frac{5}{6}$ hours to fix Mrs. Sax's car. It took $3\frac{1}{2}$ hours to fix Mr. Wong's car. How long did it take to fix both cars?

It took _____ hours to fix both cars.

4.

Perfect score: 4   My score: _____

114

Lesson 9 Addition

Write each answer in simplest form.

	a	b	c	d

1.
   $\frac{1}{12}$ $5\frac{5}{6}$ $4\frac{1}{3}$ $\frac{9}{16}$

   $+\frac{1}{6}$ $+3\frac{5}{8}$ $+2\frac{3}{4}$ $+\frac{3}{4}$

2.
   $1\frac{1}{4}$ $\frac{4}{7}$ $3\frac{3}{4}$ $\frac{7}{18}$

   $+6\frac{3}{5}$ $+\frac{9}{10}$ $+\frac{9}{10}$ $+\frac{7}{9}$

3.
   $\frac{5}{7}$ $4\frac{2}{5}$ $\frac{5}{12}$ $\frac{9}{14}$

   $+\frac{1}{2}$ $+2\frac{8}{15}$ $+5\frac{3}{4}$ $+\frac{2}{7}$

4.
   $2\frac{1}{10}$ $\frac{1}{12}$ $\frac{5}{6}$ $8\frac{1}{3}$

   $+1\frac{1}{6}$ $+\frac{5}{9}$ $+\frac{1}{2}$ $+3\frac{2}{9}$

5.
   $\frac{2}{5}$ $\frac{7}{9}$ $5\frac{2}{5}$ $7\frac{3}{4}$

   $+\frac{3}{10}$ $+1\frac{1}{6}$ $+3\frac{7}{10}$ $+9\frac{5}{6}$

Perfect score: 20   My score: _____

Problem Solving

Solve. Write each answer in simplest form.

1. Clyde weighs $71\frac{1}{4}$ pounds. His sister weighs $10\frac{3}{4}$ pounds more than that. How much does his sister weigh?

His sister weighs _____ pounds.

2. Arlene spent $2\frac{1}{2}$ hours planting part of a garden. It took her $1\frac{3}{4}$ hours to finish planting the garden. How long did it take to plant the garden?

It took _____ hours.

3. A basket weighs $1\frac{1}{8}$ pounds when empty. Jake put $10\frac{1}{2}$ pounds of apples in the basket. How much do the basket and apples weigh?

The basket and apples weigh _____ pounds.

4. June's normal body temperature is $98\frac{6}{10}°$ F. The doctor said her temperature is $2\frac{1}{2}$ degrees above normal. What is her temperature?

Her temperature is _____ ° F.

5. Ned jumped a distance of $4\frac{1}{3}$ feet. Phil jumped $1\frac{1}{4}$ feet farther than Ned. How far did Phil jump?

Phil jumped _____ feet.

6. A board $1\frac{3}{8}$ inches thick is glued to a board $1\frac{3}{4}$ inches thick. What is the combined thickness of the boards?

The combined thickness is _____ inches.

1.	2.
3.	**4.**
5.	**6.**

Perfect score: 6   My score: _____

116

Lesson 10   Addition

Write each answer in simplest form.

	a	b	c	d
1.	$\dfrac{1}{9}$ $+\dfrac{4}{9}$	$\dfrac{2}{7}$ $+\dfrac{3}{7}$	$\dfrac{8}{9}$ $+\dfrac{5}{9}$	$\dfrac{11}{16}$ $+\dfrac{7}{16}$
2.	$\dfrac{2}{3}$ $+\dfrac{1}{5}$	$\dfrac{2}{5}$ $+\dfrac{3}{4}$	$\dfrac{1}{2}$ $+\dfrac{3}{4}$	$\dfrac{5}{6}$ $+\dfrac{1}{12}$
3.	$\dfrac{7}{8}$ $+\dfrac{5}{6}$	$\dfrac{5}{12}$ $+\dfrac{1}{3}$	$\dfrac{1}{5}$ $+\dfrac{7}{10}$	$\dfrac{7}{8}$ $+\dfrac{5}{12}$
4.	$\dfrac{2}{5}$ $+\dfrac{1}{5}$	$2\dfrac{1}{9}$ $+\dfrac{1}{3}$	$7\dfrac{5}{8}$ $+\dfrac{2}{3}$	$4\dfrac{7}{12}$ $+1\dfrac{1}{2}$
5.	$\dfrac{1}{5}$ $+\dfrac{1}{3}$	$\dfrac{3}{4}$ $+\dfrac{1}{5}$	$1\dfrac{2}{3}$ $+1\dfrac{5}{6}$	$3\dfrac{11}{12}$ $+2\dfrac{5}{6}$

Perfect score: 20   My score: _____

Problem Solving

Solve. Write each answer in simplest form.

1. Jack lives $\frac{7}{8}$ mile from the stadium and $\frac{3}{8}$ mile from the school. He walked home from school and then to the stadium. How far did he walk?

Jack walked _____ miles.

2. Peggy read $\frac{5}{6}$ hour before dinner. After dinner she read $\frac{2}{5}$ hour. How long did she read?

Peggy read _____ hours in all.

3. The Clements family drank $\frac{3}{4}$ gallon of milk for dinner. There was $\frac{1}{2}$ gallon left. How much milk was there before dinner?

There was _____ gallon of milk.

4. Gary rides the bus $1\frac{3}{10}$ miles every day. Glen rides $\frac{3}{10}$ mile farther than Gary. How far does Glen ride?

Glen rides _____ miles every day.

5. June is $4\frac{3}{4}$ feet tall. Her father is $1\frac{1}{2}$ feet taller than that. How tall is June's father?

He is _____ feet tall.

6. To make pale blue paint, Lynn mixed $2\frac{1}{4}$ gallons of blue paint and $3\frac{3}{4}$ gallons of white paint. How much pale blue paint did she make?

She made _____ gallons of pale blue paint.

7. Last year Becky was $49\frac{1}{2}$ inches tall. Since then she has grown $1\frac{7}{8}$ inches. How tall is she now?

She is now _____ inches tall.

1.	
2.	**3.**
4.	**5.**
6.	**7.**

Perfect score: 7   My score: _____

118

CHAPTER 10 TEST

Write each answer in simplest form.

	a	b	c	d
1.	$\dfrac{3}{10}$ $+\dfrac{1}{10}$	$\dfrac{5}{6}$ $+\dfrac{1}{6}$	$\dfrac{7}{8}$ $+\dfrac{5}{8}$	$\dfrac{4}{7}$ $+\dfrac{1}{7}$
2.	$\dfrac{5}{8}$ $+\dfrac{1}{4}$	$\dfrac{3}{10}$ $+\dfrac{3}{4}$	$\dfrac{1}{2}$ $+\dfrac{4}{5}$	$\dfrac{5}{6}$ $+\dfrac{3}{4}$
3.	$5\dfrac{3}{10}$ $+1\dfrac{1}{3}$	$4\dfrac{2}{9}$ $+2\dfrac{2}{3}$	$\dfrac{5}{6}$ $+3\dfrac{1}{12}$	$6\dfrac{5}{12}$ $+\ \dfrac{1}{3}$
4.	$1\dfrac{3}{4}$ $+4\dfrac{7}{10}$	$5\dfrac{1}{3}$ $+\ \dfrac{4}{5}$	$2\dfrac{3}{4}$ $+6\dfrac{15}{16}$	$7\dfrac{7}{10}$ $+8\dfrac{4}{5}$
5.	$7\dfrac{1}{5}$ $+\ \dfrac{1}{4}$	$9\dfrac{9}{10}$ $+\ \dfrac{7}{12}$	$42\dfrac{5}{6}$ $+\ 5\dfrac{2}{3}$	$54\dfrac{1}{2}$ $+21\dfrac{4}{5}$

10

Perfect score: 20   My score: _____

119

Write each answer in simplest form.

	a	b	c	d
1.	$\dfrac{7}{8}$ $-\dfrac{3}{8}$	$\dfrac{8}{9}$ $-\dfrac{2}{9}$	$\dfrac{5}{6}$ $-\dfrac{1}{6}$	$\dfrac{11}{12}$ $-\dfrac{3}{12}$
2.	$5\dfrac{4}{5}$ $-2\dfrac{1}{5}$	$4\dfrac{5}{9}$ $-3\dfrac{2}{9}$	$6\dfrac{4}{7}$ $-1\dfrac{6}{7}$	$3\dfrac{3}{8}$ $-\dfrac{7}{8}$
3.	$\dfrac{5}{6}$ $-\dfrac{2}{3}$	$\dfrac{2}{3}$ $-\dfrac{1}{2}$	$\dfrac{8}{9}$ $-\dfrac{1}{3}$	$\dfrac{7}{8}$ $-\dfrac{3}{4}$
4.	$\dfrac{7}{10}$ $-\dfrac{1}{5}$	$\dfrac{7}{8}$ $-\dfrac{3}{10}$	$\dfrac{9}{10}$ $-\dfrac{2}{5}$	$\dfrac{5}{6}$ $-\dfrac{7}{12}$
5.	$4\dfrac{5}{6}$ $-2\dfrac{1}{3}$	$3\dfrac{7}{8}$ $-1\dfrac{2}{3}$	$2\dfrac{1}{10}$ $-1\dfrac{4}{5}$	$2\dfrac{1}{5}$ $-\dfrac{2}{3}$

Perfect score: 20   My score: _____

Lesson 1 Subtraction

Study how to subtract when fractions have the same denominator.

Subtract the numerators.

$$\frac{7}{8} - \frac{5}{8} = \frac{7-5}{8} = \frac{2}{8} = \frac{1}{4}$$

Use the same denominator.   Change to simplest form.

Subtract the numerators.

$$\begin{array}{r} \frac{7}{8} \\ -\frac{5}{8} \\ \hline \frac{2}{8} = \frac{1}{4} \end{array}$$

Use the same denominator.

Change to simplest form.

Write each answer in simplest form.

	a	b	c	d	e
1.	$\begin{array}{r}\frac{5}{9}\\-\frac{4}{9}\\\hline\end{array}$	$\begin{array}{r}\frac{3}{5}\\-\frac{1}{5}\\\hline\end{array}$	$\begin{array}{r}\frac{8}{9}\\-\frac{4}{9}\\\hline\end{array}$	$\begin{array}{r}\frac{3}{4}\\-\frac{1}{4}\\\hline\end{array}$	$\begin{array}{r}\frac{5}{6}\\-\frac{1}{6}\\\hline\end{array}$
2.	$\begin{array}{r}\frac{6}{7}\\-\frac{4}{7}\\\hline\end{array}$	$\begin{array}{r}\frac{5}{8}\\-\frac{3}{8}\\\hline\end{array}$	$\begin{array}{r}\frac{9}{10}\\-\frac{3}{10}\\\hline\end{array}$	$\begin{array}{r}\frac{2}{5}\\-\frac{1}{5}\\\hline\end{array}$	$\begin{array}{r}\frac{5}{9}\\-\frac{1}{9}\\\hline\end{array}$
3.	$\begin{array}{r}\frac{5}{7}\\-\frac{2}{7}\\\hline\end{array}$	$\begin{array}{r}\frac{8}{9}\\-\frac{1}{9}\\\hline\end{array}$	$\begin{array}{r}\frac{7}{8}\\-\frac{3}{8}\\\hline\end{array}$	$\begin{array}{r}\frac{7}{12}\\-\frac{5}{12}\\\hline\end{array}$	$\begin{array}{r}\frac{9}{10}\\-\frac{7}{10}\\\hline\end{array}$
4.	$\begin{array}{r}\frac{4}{5}\\-\frac{2}{5}\\\hline\end{array}$	$\begin{array}{r}\frac{2}{3}\\-\frac{1}{3}\\\hline\end{array}$	$\begin{array}{r}\frac{7}{10}\\-\frac{3}{10}\\\hline\end{array}$	$\begin{array}{r}\frac{7}{9}\\-\frac{4}{9}\\\hline\end{array}$	$\begin{array}{r}\frac{7}{8}\\-\frac{1}{8}\\\hline\end{array}$

Perfect score: 20   My score: _____

Lesson 2 Subtraction

Rename the whole number as a mixed numeral so
the denominator is the same as that of the fraction.

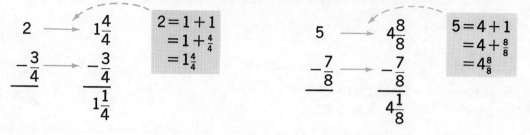

Write each answer in simplest form.

	a	*b*	*c*	*d*
1.	2	3	6	5
	$-\dfrac{1}{4}$	$-\dfrac{2}{3}$	$-\dfrac{1}{5}$	$-\dfrac{1}{3}$
2.	4	5	4	6
	$-\dfrac{3}{4}$	$-\dfrac{2}{5}$	$-\dfrac{2}{5}$	$-\dfrac{5}{6}$
3.	1	2	1	2
	$-\dfrac{1}{2}$	$-\dfrac{7}{8}$	$-\dfrac{1}{8}$	$-\dfrac{3}{10}$

Perfect score: 12   My score: _____

Lesson 3 Subtraction

$\frac{1}{4}$ is less than $\frac{3}{4}$. So
rename $7\frac{1}{4}$ as shown so
you can subtract the
fractions.

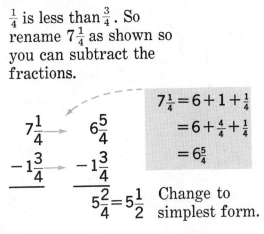

$$7\frac{1}{4} = 6 + 1 + \frac{1}{4}$$
$$= 6 + \frac{4}{4} + \frac{1}{4}$$
$$= 6\frac{5}{4}$$

$5\frac{2}{4} = 5\frac{1}{2}$ Change to
simplest form.

$\frac{1}{3}$ is less than $\frac{2}{3}$. So
rename $3\frac{1}{3}$ as shown so
you can subtract the
fractions.

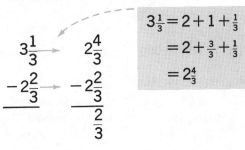

$$3\frac{1}{3} = 2 + 1 + \frac{1}{3}$$
$$= 2 + \frac{3}{3} + \frac{1}{3}$$
$$= 2\frac{4}{3}$$

Write each answer in simplest form.

	a	*b*	*c*	*d*
1.	$5\frac{8}{9}$ $-2\frac{6}{9}$	$4\frac{6}{7}$ $-2\frac{1}{7}$	$8\frac{9}{10}$ $-3\frac{4}{10}$	$6\frac{3}{8}$ $-2\frac{1}{8}$
2.	$5\frac{1}{3}$ $-1\frac{2}{3}$	$7\frac{2}{5}$ $-1\frac{4}{5}$	$8\frac{3}{8}$ $-2\frac{5}{8}$	$6\frac{1}{9}$ $-2\frac{6}{9}$
3.	$5\frac{3}{12}$ $-2\frac{11}{12}$	$4\frac{5}{6}$ $-2\frac{2}{6}$	$3\frac{2}{5}$ $-1\frac{4}{5}$	$7\frac{2}{3}$ $-6\frac{2}{3}$

Perfect score: 12   My score: _____

Problem Solving

Solve. Write each answer in simplest form.

1. A board is 8 feet long. Hank said that this board is $2\frac{1}{2}$ feet too long for the job. How long a board does Hank need?

He needs a board _____ feet long.

2. Sue says it will take $6\frac{1}{6}$ hours to travel to her grandparents' home. She has been traveling $3\frac{5}{6}$ hours. How much longer will it be before she gets there?

It will be _____ hours longer.

3. The stakes in Don's croquet set are 2 feet long. He drove one stake $\frac{3}{4}$ foot into the ground. How much of the stake is above the ground?

_____ feet are above the ground.

4. An envelope is 7 inches wide. A sheet of paper is $6\frac{1}{2}$ inches wide. How much wider than the paper is the envelope?

It is _____ inch wider.

5. This year Reola spends $5\frac{1}{4}$ hours in school each day. Last year she spent $4\frac{3}{4}$ hours in school each day. How many more hours does she spend in school each day this year than last year?

She spends _____ hour more in school each day this year than last year.

6. A wire is $4\frac{7}{12}$ feet long. Suppose $\frac{11}{12}$ foot of wire is used. How much wire would be left?

_____ feet of wire would be left.

1.	2.
3.	**4.**
5.	**6.**

Perfect score: 6   My score: _____

124

Lesson 4 Subtraction

When subtracting fractions that have different denominators, rename the fractions so they have the same denominator.

$$\begin{array}{r} \dfrac{2}{3} \times \dfrac{4}{4} = \dfrac{8}{12} \\ -\dfrac{1}{4} \times \dfrac{3}{3} = -\dfrac{3}{12} \\ \hline \dfrac{5}{12} \end{array}$$

Since $3 \times 4 = 12$, rename each fraction with a denominator of 12.

$$\begin{array}{r} \dfrac{5}{6} \longrightarrow \dfrac{5}{6} \\ -\dfrac{1}{2} \times \dfrac{3}{3} = -\dfrac{3}{6} \\ \hline \dfrac{2}{6} = \dfrac{1}{3} \end{array}$$

Since $2 \times 3 = 6$, rename only $\frac{1}{2}$ with a denominator of 6.

Write each answer in simplest form.

	a	b	c	d
1.	$\dfrac{3}{5}$ $-\dfrac{1}{3}$	$\dfrac{5}{6}$ $-\dfrac{2}{5}$	$\dfrac{7}{8}$ $-\dfrac{1}{2}$	$\dfrac{2}{3}$ $-\dfrac{4}{9}$
2.	$\dfrac{5}{6}$ $-\dfrac{1}{3}$	$\dfrac{2}{3}$ $-\dfrac{1}{6}$	$\dfrac{7}{12}$ $-\dfrac{1}{4}$	$\dfrac{4}{5}$ $-\dfrac{3}{10}$
3.	$\dfrac{9}{10}$ $-\dfrac{1}{2}$	$\dfrac{5}{6}$ $-\dfrac{3}{7}$	$\dfrac{3}{4}$ $-\dfrac{1}{5}$	$\dfrac{11}{12}$ $-\dfrac{1}{6}$

Perfect score: 12   My score: _____

Problem Solving

Solve. Write each answer in simplest form.

1. Phillip jogged $\frac{5}{6}$ mile. He walked $\frac{1}{2}$ mile. How much farther did he jog than he walked?

He jogged _____ mile farther than he walked.

2. Eddie and Johnnie have painted $\frac{2}{3}$ of a room. Eddie painted $\frac{1}{2}$ of the room. How much of the room did Johnnie paint?

Johnnie painted _____ of the room.

3. Millie and Joan have $\frac{5}{6}$ of a room painted. Joan painted $\frac{1}{5}$ of the room. How much of the room did Millie paint?

Millie painted _____ of the room.

4. Ardith had $\frac{3}{4}$ dozen eggs. She used $\frac{7}{12}$ dozen for breakfast. How many dozen did she have left?

She has _____ dozen eggs left.

5. A rock weighs $\frac{9}{16}$ pound. Suppose $\frac{1}{4}$ pound is chipped away. How much would the remaining rock weigh?

The remaining part would weigh _____ pound.

6. It takes Barbara $\frac{5}{6}$ hour to get to work. In doing so, she rides the train $\frac{2}{3}$ hour. She walks the remaining time. How much time does she spend walking to work?

She spends _____ hour walking to work.

7. Mr. Anthony and Mr. Androtti completed $\frac{3}{4}$ of a job. Mr. Androtti completed $\frac{2}{9}$ of the job. What part of the job did Mr. Anthony complete?

Mr. Anthony completed _____ of the job.

1.
2.
3.
4.
5.
6.
7.

Perfect score: 7   My score: _____

Lesson 5   Subtraction

$$\frac{3}{4} \longrightarrow \frac{15}{20}$$
$$-\frac{3}{5} \longrightarrow -\frac{12}{20}$$
$$\frac{3}{20}$$

$$\frac{9}{10} \longrightarrow \frac{27}{30}$$
$$-\frac{11}{15} \longrightarrow -\frac{22}{30}$$
$$\frac{5}{30} = \frac{1}{6}$$

Write each answer in simplest form.

	a	b	c	d
1.	$\frac{5}{6}$ $-\frac{3}{8}$	$\frac{3}{4}$ $-\frac{1}{6}$	$\frac{7}{8}$ $-\frac{3}{10}$	$\frac{5}{6}$ $-\frac{2}{9}$
2.	$\frac{9}{10}$ $-\frac{3}{5}$	$\frac{7}{8}$ $-\frac{1}{6}$	$\frac{2}{3}$ $-\frac{1}{5}$	$\frac{8}{9}$ $-\frac{5}{6}$
3.	$\frac{3}{4}$ $-\frac{5}{12}$	$\frac{7}{12}$ $-\frac{1}{4}$	$\frac{7}{8}$ $-\frac{1}{3}$	$\frac{3}{10}$ $-\frac{1}{4}$
4.	$\frac{2}{3}$ $-\frac{4}{9}$	$\frac{11}{12}$ $-\frac{3}{8}$	$\frac{1}{4}$ $-\frac{1}{12}$	$\frac{2}{3}$ $-\frac{7}{12}$

Perfect score: 16   My score: _____

Problem Solving

Solve. Write each answer in simplest form.

1. Who lives farther from the bank, Cal or Dot? How much farther?

_____ lives _____ mile farther.

2. Who lives farther from the bank, Ken or Cal? How much farther?

_____ lives _____ mile farther.

3. How much farther is it from Dot's house to Cal's house than from Dot's house to the bank?

It is _____ mile farther.

4. How much farther is it from Dot's house to Ken's house than from Dot's house to the bank?

It is _____ mile farther.

5. Cal walked from his house to Dot's house. Ken walked from his house to Dot's house. Who walked farther? How much farther?

_____ walked _____ mile farther.

1.	
2.	3.
4.	5.

Lesson 6   Subtraction

Rename so the fractions have the same denominator.

Rename $7\frac{3}{12}$ so you can subtract.

$$7\frac{1}{4} \longrightarrow 7\frac{3}{12} \longrightarrow 6\frac{15}{12}$$
$$-3\frac{2}{3} \longrightarrow -3\frac{8}{12} \longrightarrow -3\frac{8}{12}$$
$$\overline{} \qquad \overline{} \qquad \overline{3\frac{7}{12}}$$

$$7\frac{3}{12}=7+\frac{3}{12}$$
$$=6+1+\frac{3}{12}$$
$$=6+\frac{12}{12}+\frac{3}{12}$$
$$=6+\frac{15}{12}$$
$$=6\frac{15}{12}$$

Write each answer in simplest form.

	a	b	c	d
1.	$5\frac{1}{3}$ $-3\frac{3}{4}$	$7\frac{3}{5}$ $-4\frac{7}{10}$	$6\frac{1}{6}$ $-1\frac{3}{8}$	$5\frac{4}{9}$ $-2\frac{1}{3}$
2.	$4\frac{3}{8}$ $-2\frac{1}{3}$	$3\frac{5}{6}$ $-2\frac{1}{12}$	$6\frac{4}{7}$ $-5\frac{1}{2}$	$6\frac{3}{5}$ $-2\frac{3}{10}$
3.	$5\frac{7}{8}$ $-1\frac{3}{5}$	$3\frac{1}{9}$ $-\frac{1}{3}$	$2\frac{2}{3}$ $-1\frac{1}{2}$	$1\frac{3}{8}$ $-\frac{9}{10}$
4.	$4\frac{2}{9}$ $-\frac{2}{3}$	$6\frac{4}{5}$ $-5\frac{3}{7}$	$3\frac{7}{12}$ $-1\frac{9}{10}$	$2\frac{1}{8}$ $-\frac{5}{12}$

Perfect score: 16   My score: _____

Problem Solving

Solve. Write each answer in simplest form.

1. One fish weighed $1\frac{1}{2}$ pounds. Another weighed $\frac{3}{4}$ pound. How much more did the heavier fish weigh?

It weighed _____ pound more.

2. Mrs. Tanner bought $2\frac{1}{2}$ gallons of paint. She used $1\frac{2}{3}$ gallons of paint on the garage. How much paint did she have left?

She had _____ gallon left.

3. Lorena has two boxes that weigh a total of $4\frac{1}{2}$ pounds. One box weighs $1\frac{7}{10}$ pounds. How much does the other box weigh?

It weighs _____ pounds.

4. Allen practiced the guitar $1\frac{1}{4}$ hours today. He practiced $\frac{2}{3}$ hour before lunch. How long did he practice after lunch?

He practiced _____ hour after lunch.

5. Karen ran a race in $9\frac{3}{10}$ seconds. Curt ran the race in $7\frac{4}{5}$ seconds. How much longer did it take Karen to run the race?

It took _____ seconds longer.

6. Fido weighs $2\frac{5}{16}$ pounds. Spot weighs $4\frac{7}{8}$ pounds. How much more than Fido does Spot weigh?

Spot weighs _____ pounds more.

1.
2.
3.
4.
5.
6.

Perfect score: 6   My score: _____

130

Lesson 7 Subtraction

Write each answer in simplest form.

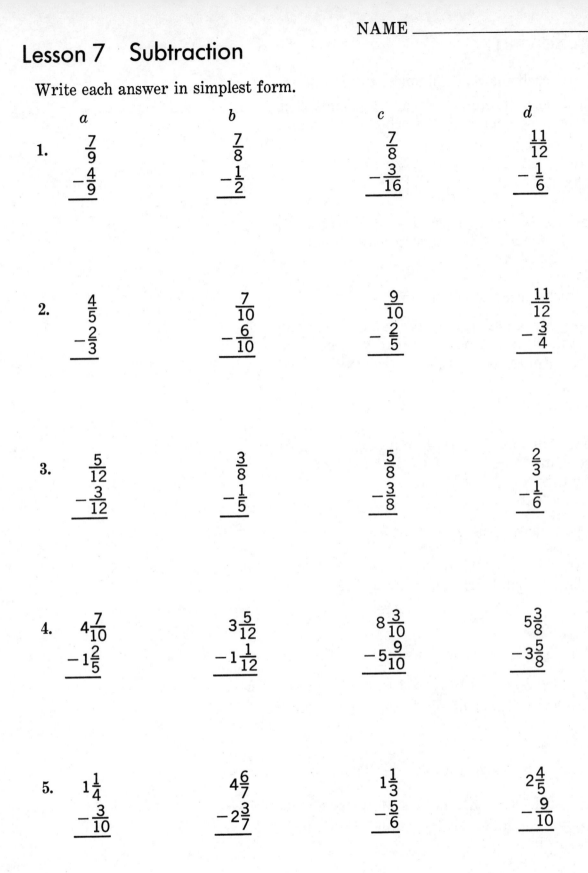

	a	b	c	d
1.	$\frac{7}{9}$ $-\frac{4}{9}$	$\frac{7}{8}$ $-\frac{1}{2}$	$\frac{7}{8}$ $-\frac{3}{16}$	$\frac{11}{12}$ $-\frac{1}{6}$
2.	$\frac{4}{5}$ $-\frac{2}{3}$	$\frac{7}{10}$ $-\frac{6}{10}$	$\frac{9}{10}$ $-\frac{2}{5}$	$\frac{11}{12}$ $-\frac{3}{4}$
3.	$\frac{5}{12}$ $-\frac{3}{12}$	$\frac{3}{8}$ $-\frac{1}{5}$	$\frac{5}{8}$ $-\frac{3}{8}$	$\frac{2}{3}$ $-\frac{1}{6}$
4.	$4\frac{7}{10}$ $-1\frac{2}{5}$	$3\frac{5}{12}$ $-1\frac{1}{12}$	$8\frac{3}{10}$ $-5\frac{9}{10}$	$5\frac{3}{8}$ $-3\frac{5}{8}$
5.	$1\frac{1}{4}$ $-\frac{3}{10}$	$4\frac{6}{7}$ $-2\frac{3}{7}$	$1\frac{1}{3}$ $-\frac{5}{6}$	$2\frac{4}{5}$ $-\frac{9}{10}$

Perfect score: 20   My score: _____

Problem Solving

Solve. Write each answer in simplest form.

1. A pail filled with water weighs $9\frac{1}{4}$ pounds. The empty pail weighs $\frac{3}{4}$ pound. How much does the water weigh?

The water weighs _____ pounds.

2. A board is $4\frac{5}{8}$ inches long. We need a piece $2\frac{7}{8}$ inches long. How much of the board needs to be cut off?

_____ inches need to be cut off.

3. John and Mary are reading the same book. John has read $\frac{4}{5}$ of the book and Mary has read $\frac{2}{3}$ of the book. How much more of the book has John read than Mary?

John has read _____ more of the book.

4. A recipe calls for $3\frac{1}{2}$ cups of flour and $1\frac{3}{4}$ cups of sugar. How many more cups of flour than sugar are called for by the recipe?

_____ cups more of flour are called for.

5. Judy worked $7\frac{1}{2}$ hours. Harry worked $5\frac{3}{4}$ hours. How much longer than Harry did Judy work?

She worked _____ hours longer.

6. It took Vera $2\frac{2}{3}$ hours to read 2 books. She read one book in $\frac{5}{6}$ hour. How long did it take her to read the other one?

It took _____ hours to read the other book.

7. Mr. Wakefield used $8\frac{1}{4}$ gallons of water to fill 2 tanks. He put $3\frac{7}{8}$ gallons in one tank. How much water did he put in the other tank?

He put _____ gallons in the other tank.

1.

2.

3.

4.

5.

6.

7.

Perfect score: 7   My score: _____

132

Lesson 8   Subtraction

Write each answer in simplest form.

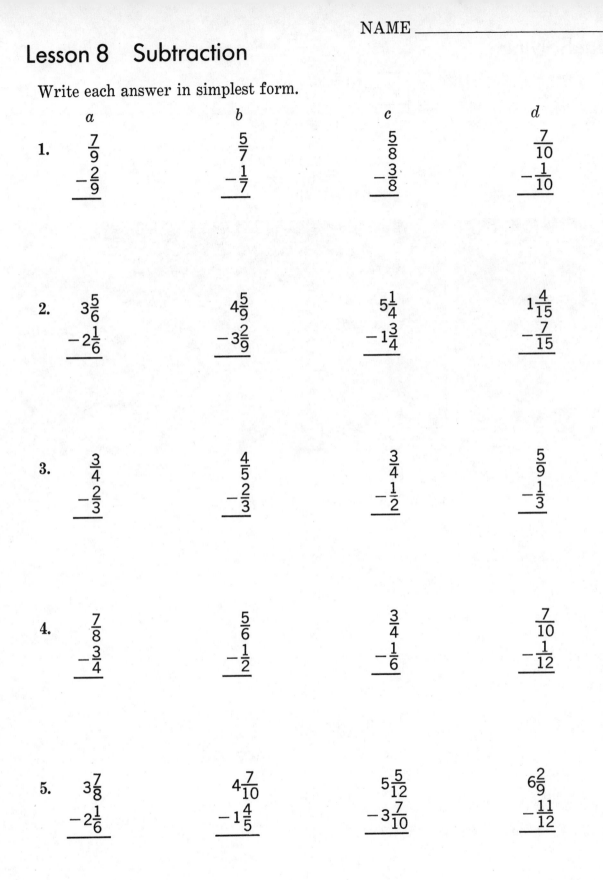

	a	b	c	d
1.	$\dfrac{7}{9}$ $-\dfrac{2}{9}$	$\dfrac{5}{7}$ $-\dfrac{1}{7}$	$\dfrac{5}{8}$ $-\dfrac{3}{8}$	$\dfrac{7}{10}$ $-\dfrac{1}{10}$
2.	$3\dfrac{5}{6}$ $-2\dfrac{1}{6}$	$4\dfrac{5}{9}$ $-3\dfrac{2}{9}$	$5\dfrac{1}{4}$ $-1\dfrac{3}{4}$	$1\dfrac{4}{15}$ $-\dfrac{7}{15}$
3.	$\dfrac{3}{4}$ $-\dfrac{2}{3}$	$\dfrac{4}{5}$ $-\dfrac{2}{3}$	$\dfrac{3}{4}$ $-\dfrac{1}{2}$	$\dfrac{5}{9}$ $-\dfrac{1}{3}$
4.	$\dfrac{7}{8}$ $-\dfrac{3}{4}$	$\dfrac{5}{6}$ $-\dfrac{1}{2}$	$\dfrac{3}{4}$ $-\dfrac{1}{6}$	$\dfrac{7}{10}$ $-\dfrac{1}{12}$
5.	$3\dfrac{7}{8}$ $-2\dfrac{1}{6}$	$4\dfrac{7}{10}$ $-1\dfrac{4}{5}$	$5\dfrac{5}{12}$ $-3\dfrac{7}{10}$	$6\dfrac{2}{9}$ $-\dfrac{11}{12}$

Perfect score: 20   My score: _____

Problem Solving

Animal	Weight
dog	$4\frac{1}{2}$ lbs
cat	$2\frac{2}{3}$ lbs
rabbit	$1\frac{3}{4}$ lbs

Solve. Write each answer in simplest form.

1. How much more does the dog weigh than the cat?

The dog weighs _____ pounds more than the cat.

2. How much more does the dog weigh than the rabbit?

The dog weighs _____ pounds more than the rabbit.

3. How much more does the cat weigh than the rabbit?

The cat weighs _____ pound more than the rabbit.

4. How much do the dog and the cat weigh together?

Together, the dog and the cat weigh _____ pounds.

1.

2.

3.

4.

Perfect score: 4   My score: _____

134

CHAPTER 11 TEST

Write each answer in simplest form.

	a	b	c	d
1.	$\dfrac{9}{10}$ $-\dfrac{7}{10}$	$\dfrac{4}{5}$ $-\dfrac{2}{3}$	$\dfrac{3}{4}$ $-\dfrac{5}{8}$	$\dfrac{8}{9}$ $-\dfrac{2}{9}$
2.	$\dfrac{5}{6}$ $-\dfrac{1}{2}$	$\dfrac{1}{2}$ $-\dfrac{3}{8}$	$\dfrac{11}{12}$ $-\dfrac{3}{12}$	$\dfrac{1}{2}$ $-\dfrac{5}{12}$
3.	$\dfrac{3}{4}$ $-\dfrac{3}{8}$	$\dfrac{5}{6}$ $-\dfrac{1}{9}$	$\dfrac{7}{8}$ $-\dfrac{1}{4}$	$\dfrac{2}{3}$ $-\dfrac{1}{2}$
4.	$5\dfrac{7}{8}$ $-2\dfrac{3}{8}$	$4\dfrac{2}{5}$ $-2\dfrac{3}{10}$	$6\dfrac{1}{2}$ $-1\dfrac{1}{3}$	$3\dfrac{1}{3}$ $-1\dfrac{5}{6}$
5.	$3\dfrac{11}{12}$ $-1\dfrac{5}{6}$	$5\dfrac{5}{8}$ $-2\dfrac{3}{4}$	$2\dfrac{1}{9}$ $-\dfrac{7}{9}$	$1\dfrac{2}{5}$ $-\dfrac{1}{2}$

Perfect score: 20   My score: _____

Circle the correct name for each figure.

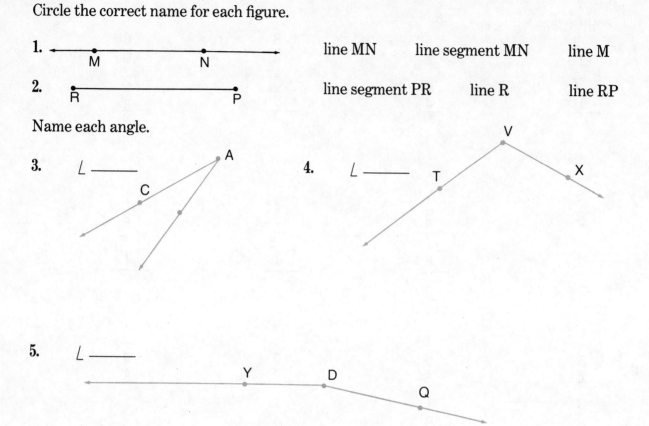

1.   line MN   line segment MN   line M

2.   line segment PR   line R   line RP

Name each angle.

3.   ∠ _____

4.   ∠ _____

5.   ∠ _____

Write the letter for the name of each figure in the blank.

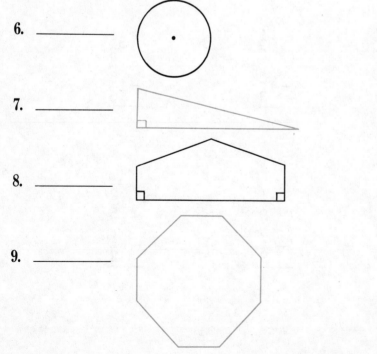

6. _____

7. _____

8. _____

9. _____

a. octagon

b. triangle

c. hexagon

d. pentagon

e. square

f. quadrilateral

g. circle

Perfect score: 9   My score: _____

136

Lesson 1   Lines and Line Segments

A **line** has no endpoints.

To name a line, name any two points on the line.

J   W

line JW   or   line WJ

A **line segment** has two **endpoints.**

A line segment is part of a line. The line segment consists of the endpoints and all points on the line between the endpoints. To name a line segment, name the endpoints.

G   S

line segment GS   or   line segment SG

Circle the correct name for each figure.

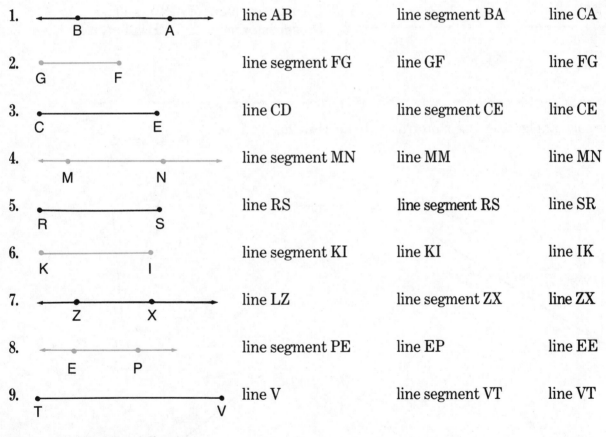

1.   line AB   line segment BA   line CA
   B   A

2.   line segment FG   line GF   line FG
   G   F

3.   line CD   line segment CE   line CE
   C   E

4.   line segment MN   line MM   line MN
   M   N

5.   line RS   line segment RS   line SR
   R   S

6.   line segment KI   line KI   line IK
   K   I

7.   line LZ   line segment ZX   line ZX
   Z   X

8.   line segment PE   line EP   line EE
   E   P

9.   line V   line segment VT   line VT
   T   V

Draw and label the following.

10. line segment HQ

Lesson 2   Angles

An **angle** has two sides and a **vertex**.

Angle GHB (denoted ∠GHB) has a vertex of
H. When naming an angle, use the vertex
as the middle letter.

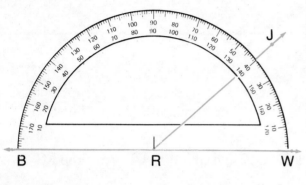

To use a protractor to measure an angle:

Place the center of the protractor at the vertex of
the angle. Align one side of the angle with the
base of the protractor. Use the scale starting at 0
and read the measure of the angle.

The measurement of ∠JRW is 40°.
The measurement of ∠JRB is 140°.

Name each angle. Then use a protractor to measure each angle.

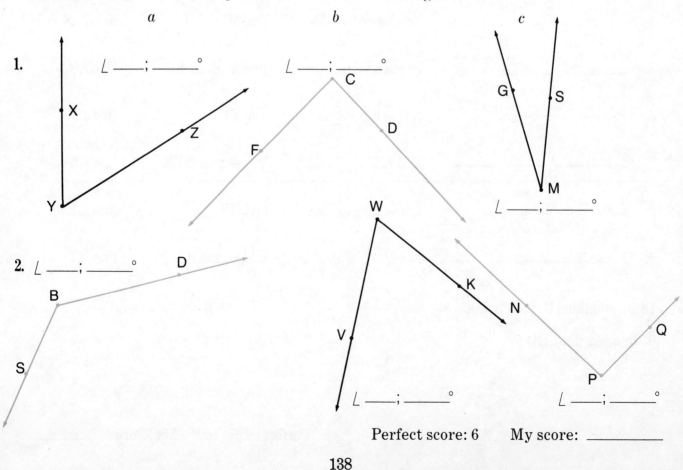

     a   *b*   *c*

1. ∠ ____ ; ____ °   ∠ ____ ; ____ °   ∠ ____ ; ____ °

2. ∠ ____ ; ____ °

Perfect score: 6   My score: _____

138

Lesson 3   Polygons

Polygons are named for the number of sides they have.

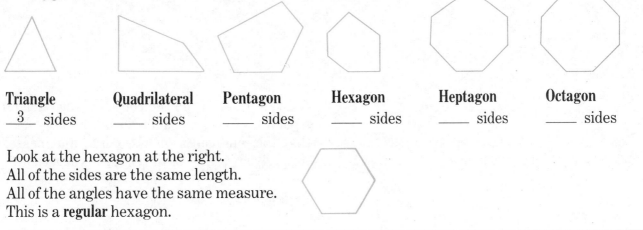

Triangle	**Quadrilateral**	**Pentagon**	**Hexagon**	**Heptagon**	**Octagon**
_3_ sides	___ sides	___ sides	___ sides	___ sides	___ sides

Look at the hexagon at the right.
All of the sides are the same length.
All of the angles have the same measure.
This is a **regular** hexagon.

On the line after each name, write the letter(s) of the figure(s) it describes. Some names will have more than one letter. Some figures have more than one name.

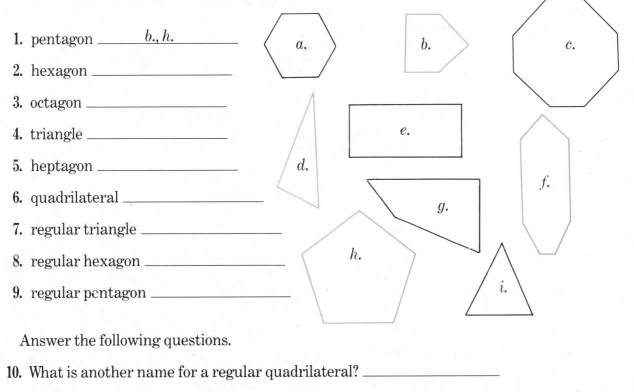

1. pentagon _____ _b., h._____
2. hexagon _____
3. octagon _____
4. triangle _____
5. heptagon _____
6. quadrilateral _____
7. regular triangle _____
8. regular hexagon _____
9. regular pentagon _____

Answer the following questions.

10. What is another name for a regular quadrilateral? _____

11. Which of the triangles shown below are **regular** triangles? _____

Perfect score: 15   My score: _____

139

Lesson 4 Polygons and Circles

To name a **polygon**, use the letters of the vertices (plural of **vertex**).

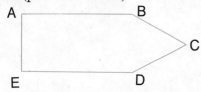

Figure ABCDE or Pentagon ABCDE

A line segment that connects two vertices, but is not a side, is called a **diagonal**.

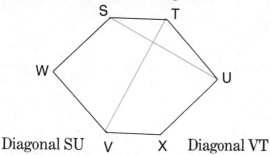

Diagonal SU   Diagonal VT

To name a **circle**, use the letter of the center.

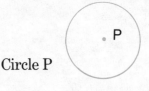

Circle P

A line segment from the center of the circle to a point on the circle is a **radius**. A line segment that has endpoints on the circle and passes through the center of the circle is a **diameter**.

Radius LM

Diameter KN

Note that KL and LN are also **radii** (plural of radius).

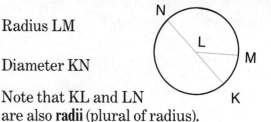

---

1. Draw and name all of the diagonals of figure FGHIJ.

   _____

2. Are all of the diagonals of figure FGHIJ the same length? _____

3. Name a radius of circle P. _____

4. Name a diameter of circle P. _____

5. In circle P, draw a diameter that goes through point N.

6. Is figure RSTUVW a regular hexagon? _____

7. Draw all the diagonals for figure RSTUVW.

8. How many diagonals does figure RSTUVW have? _____

9. Are all of the diagonals of figure RSTUVW the same length? _____

Perfect score: 9   My score: _____

Lesson 5   Three-Dimensional Objects

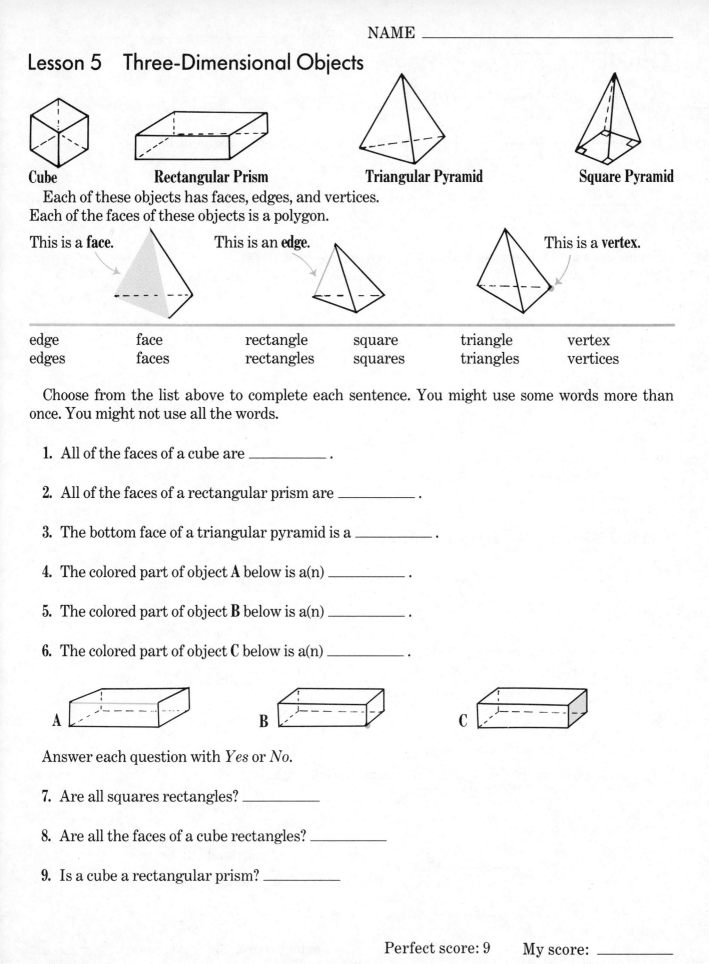

Cube   **Rectangular Prism**   **Triangular Pyramid**   **Square Pyramid**

Each of these objects has faces, edges, and vertices.
Each of the faces of these objects is a polygon.

This is a **face**.   This is an **edge**.   This is a **vertex**.

edge	face	rectangle	square	triangle	vertex
edges	faces	rectangles	squares	triangles	vertices

Choose from the list above to complete each sentence. You might use some words more than once. You might not use all the words.

1. All of the faces of a cube are _____ .

2. All of the faces of a rectangular prism are _____ .

3. The bottom face of a triangular pyramid is a _____ .

4. The colored part of object **A** below is a(n) _____ .

5. The colored part of object **B** below is a(n) _____ .

6. The colored part of object **C** below is a(n) _____ .

A   B   C

Answer each question with *Yes* or *No*.

7. Are all squares rectangles? _____

8. Are all the faces of a cube rectangles? _____

9. Is a cube a rectangular prism? _____

Perfect score: 9   My score: _____

CHAPTER 12 TEST

Choose the correct name for each figure.

1. 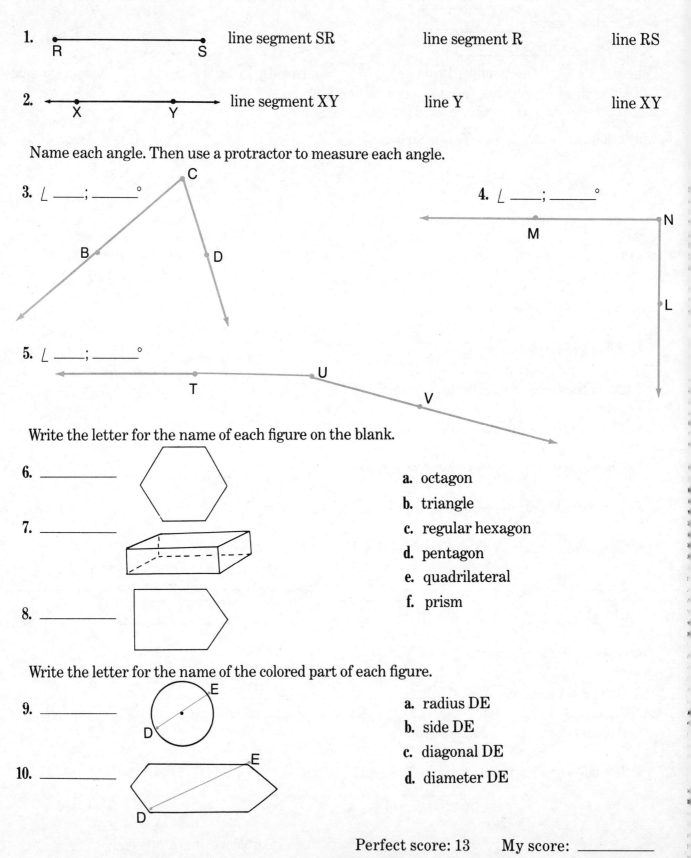   line segment SR   line segment R   line RS

2. line segment XY   line Y   line XY

Name each angle. Then use a protractor to measure each angle.

3. ∠ ____; ____°

4. ∠ ____; ____°

5. ∠ ____; ____°

Write the letter for the name of each figure on the blank.

6. _____

7. _____

8. _____

a. octagon
b. triangle
c. regular hexagon
d. pentagon
e. quadrilateral
f. prism

Write the letter for the name of the colored part of each figure.

9. _____

10. _____

a. radius DE
b. side DE
c. diagonal DE
d. diameter DE

Perfect score: 13   My score: _____

TEST—Chapters 1–7

Solve each problem.

	a	b	c	d
1.	42 +51	92 +78	134 +939	46821 93289 +25394
2.	75 −18	236 −57	1043 −389	35670 −34398
3.	78 ×5	147 ×9	850 ×8	3780 ×10
4.	37 ×28	92 ×40	248 ×75	1569 ×136
5.	6⟌96	8⟌984	9⟌3198	73⟌7338

Continued on the next page.

Test—Chapters 1–7 (Continued)

	a	*b*	*c*	*d*
6.	5$\overline{)9\ 2}$	4$\overline{)2\ 4\ 8}$	49$\overline{)1\ 6\ 8\ 2}$	89$\overline{)1\ 7\ 5\ 3\ 9}$

	a	*b*	*c*	*d*
7.	14$\overline{)9\ 8}$	9$\overline{)1\ 8\ 6}$	81$\overline{)2\ 7\ 3\ 4}$	53$\overline{)6\ 9\ 7\ 9\ 1}$

Complete the following.

	a	*b*
8.	180 cm = _____ mm	3,000 liters = _____ kl
9.	21 g = _____ mg	300 kg = _____ g
10.	36 in. = _____ yd	1 mi 200 yd = _____ yd
11.	6 gal = _____ qt	8 lb 2 oz = _____ oz

Find the perimeter and area of each figure.

a

12. perimeter = _____ ft

area = _____ square feet

3 ft

6 ft

b

perimeter = _____ centimeters

area = _____ square centimeters

40 cm

90 cm

Perfect score: 40   My score: _____

FINAL TEST—Chapters 1–12

Solve each problem.

	a	*b*	*c*	*d*	*e*
1.	3 6 +5 7	8 3 +7 9	7 9 8 +1 3 5	4 5 6 7 8 +8 2 9 0 2	7 3 1 4 6 4 5 2 9 7 1 5 + 7 2 6
2.	6 3 −1 8	1 7 8 −6 5	1 2 7 0 − 9 8 2	5 9 2 4 6 −3 7 0 9 5	7 6 0 0 5 −9 1 4 6
3.	7 3 ×6	1 2 4 ×8	7 8 5 ×5	3 8 7 ×1 0	4 2 0 ×3 2
4.	3 6 ×2 7	5 9 ×4 0	6 5 7 ×8 9	5 2 6 ×1 5 4	2 9 8 4 × 6 9 7

	a	*b*	*c*	*d*
5.	6⟌7 8	8⟌9 2 8	9⟌3 7 2 9	51⟌6 1 8 2
6.	5⟌9 7	4⟌2 3 1	45⟌9 3 5	93⟌2 7 6 5 8

Continued on the next page.

Final Test

Final Test (Continued)

	a	*b*	*c*	*d*

7. $13\overline{)9\ 3}$ $7\overline{)8\ 2\ 1}$ $68\overline{)1\ 7\ 8\ 3}$ $13\overline{)5\ 9\ 6\ 7\ 1}$

8. $25\overline{)9\ 0}$ $18\overline{)3\ 7\ 8}$ $32\overline{)3\ 1\ 8\ 5}$ $72\overline{)2\ 9\ 4\ 5\ 0}$

Complete the following.

         a   *b*

9. 160 cm = _____ mm   6 km = _____ m

10. 17 liters = _____ ml   9,000 liters = _____ kl

11. 9 g = _____ mg   30 kg = _____ g

12. 36 in. = _____ ft   1 mi 25 ft = _____ ft

13. 2 yd = _____ in.   2 qt 1 pt = _____ pt

14. 3 gal = _____ qt   6 lb 6 oz = _____ oz

Find the perimeter and area of each figure.

         a   *b*

15. perimeter = _____ ft   perimeter = _____ meters

    area = _____ square feet   area = _____ square meters

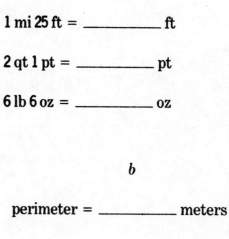

Continued on the next page.

Final Test (Continued)

Change each fraction or mixed numeral to simplest form.

a	b	c
16. $\dfrac{9}{27}$	$\dfrac{24}{30}$	$\dfrac{35}{8}$
17. $6\dfrac{4}{6}$	$1\dfrac{7}{3}$	$9\dfrac{16}{12}$

Write each answer in simplest form.

a	b	c
18. $\dfrac{2}{3} \times \dfrac{1}{5}$	$\dfrac{7}{8} \times \dfrac{1}{3}$	$\dfrac{2}{7} \times \dfrac{3}{5}$
19. $1\dfrac{1}{3} \times \dfrac{2}{5}$	$\dfrac{3}{4} \times 2\dfrac{3}{6}$	$2\dfrac{2}{3} \times 3\dfrac{3}{8}$
20. $3 \times \dfrac{5}{6}$	$1\dfrac{2}{3} \times 6$	$2\dfrac{1}{2} \times 3\dfrac{1}{3}$
21. $\dfrac{7}{10} \times 5$	$3\dfrac{7}{8} \times 16$	$4\dfrac{2}{5} \times 2\dfrac{3}{11}$

a	b	c	d
22. $\dfrac{3}{5}$ $+\dfrac{1}{5}$	$\dfrac{2}{7}$ $+\dfrac{3}{7}$	$\dfrac{5}{8}$ $+\dfrac{1}{8}$	$\dfrac{3}{10}$ $+\dfrac{3}{10}$
23. $1\dfrac{3}{8}$ $+2\dfrac{1}{8}$	$13\dfrac{4}{9}$ $+7\dfrac{8}{9}$	$\dfrac{3}{5}$ $+\dfrac{1}{2}$	$\dfrac{7}{8}$ $+\dfrac{1}{4}$
24. $\dfrac{5}{12}$ $+\dfrac{3}{4}$	$\dfrac{9}{10}$ $+\dfrac{2}{3}$	$7\dfrac{2}{5}$ $+2\dfrac{1}{10}$	$12\dfrac{3}{4}$ $+9\dfrac{2}{3}$

Continued on the next page.

Final Test (Continued)

Write each answer in simplest form.

	a	*b*	*c*	*d*
25.	$\dfrac{7}{10}$ $-\dfrac{3}{10}$	7 $-\dfrac{3}{5}$	$6\dfrac{3}{4}$ $-2\dfrac{1}{4}$	$9\dfrac{1}{8}$ $-4\dfrac{7}{8}$
26.	$\dfrac{7}{8}$ $-\dfrac{1}{4}$	$\dfrac{5}{6}$ $-\dfrac{2}{9}$	$4\dfrac{7}{8}$ $-3\dfrac{2}{3}$	$6\dfrac{9}{10}$ $-1\dfrac{7}{8}$
27.	$\dfrac{11}{12}$ $-\dfrac{3}{4}$	$\dfrac{9}{10}$ $-\dfrac{2}{3}$	$2\dfrac{1}{3}$ $-\dfrac{7}{8}$	$9\dfrac{1}{4}$ $-6\dfrac{2}{5}$

Name each figure.

28. _____

29. _____

30. _____

31. _____

32. _____

33. _____

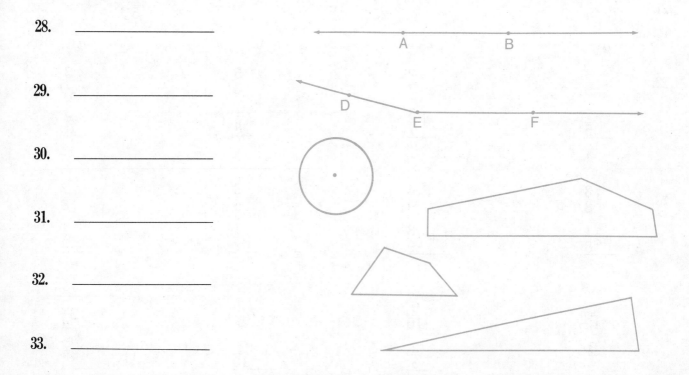

Answers
Math - Grade 5
(Answers for Pre-Tests and Tests are given on pages 155–157.)

Page 3

	a	b	c	d	e	f	g	h
1.	9	11	7	14	7	14	10	11
2.	11	14	16	5	13	10	8	12
3.	16	12	9	6	12	11	10	9
4.	10	15	10	14	17	6	5	8
5.	11	10	8	11	7	13	8	12
6.	13	9	5	12	15	14	10	17
7.	9	9	15	4	9	15	10	7
8.	8	16	10	13	13	7	7	11
9.	7	12	18	12	8	11	13	8

Page 4

	a	b	c	d	e	f	g	h
1.	5	6	4	5	7	7	6	8
2.	5	7	7	5	4	4	4	9
3.	8	4	7	3	2	8	5	6
4.	7	9	7	7	7	9	8	4
5.	6	4	8	9	6	1	2	8
6.	1	8	6	2	6	9	6	4
7.	5	1	3	8	9	8	4	9
8.	8	5	2	1	3	2	9	3
9.	5	2	6	9	3	3	7	3

Page 5

	a	b	c	d	e	f
1.	77	88	88	97	57	69
2.	62	75	91	80	84	65
3.	125	143	111	151	132	103
4.	63	68	154	105	80	110
5.	52	15	26	51	34	19
6.	69	19	25	17	18	27
7.	89	48	68	96	69	68

Page 6

1. 36 ; 47 ; 83
2. 85 ; 76 ; 9
3. 161
4. 103 ; 35 ; 68
5. 32

Page 7

	a	b	c	d	e	f
1.	796	895	860	694	827	909
2.	1185	1477	1015	852	1245	1191
3.	1605	1525	1221	1117	1211	1104
4.	422	522	228	527	585	282
5.	920	651	839	716	1256	1198
6.	885	589	893	1386	1273	1390
7.	1622	1492	509	1195	1237	1297

Page 8

1. subtract ; 177
2. add ; 942
3. add ; 1751
4. subtract ; 199
5. subtract ; 1207

Page 9

	a	b	c
1.	34984	56139	81730
2.	58349	42804	118133
3.	67115	85899	55001
4.	47226	65628	79089

Page 10

1. 4378
2. 21917
3. 4939
4. 46089
5. 39743
6. 172800
7. 20200

Page 11

	a	b	c	d	e
1.	989	973	778	2068	1495
2.	16093	12600	9882	177322	120611
3.	1225	2409	18976	138081	296013
4.	2808	7566	22183	286017	173691
5.	2611	7551	108531	124728	56635

Page 12

1. 1709
2. 1540
3. 44114
4. 44749
5. 83015
6. 52021
7. 62737

Page 15

	a	b	c	d	e	f	g	h
1.	8	16	14	4	12	10	6	2
2.	24	6	27	18	15	0	12	9
3.	8	4	24	32	28	12	36	16
4.	35	25	10	30	20	45	15	40
5.	36	12	54	18	6	42	30	48
6.	7	21	63	14	42	49	56	35
7.	40	8	56	16	72	48	24	64
8.	72	18	9	54	63	36	45	81
9.	0	0	0	0	6	2	9	7

Page 16

1. 6 ; 8 ; 48
2. 9 ; 7 ; 63
3. 8 ; 9 ; 72
4. 6 ; 7 ; 42
5. 64
6. 45

Page 17

	a	b	c	d	e	f
1.	64	63	84	264	639	842
2.	64	72	84	492	381	860
3.	219	168	405	704	688	789
4.	285	168	148	768	770	885
5.	168	376	195	2982	2148	1170
6.	456	96	350	1578	2045	5110
7.	648	665	648	5032	5607	5922

Page 18

1. 32 ; 3 ; 96
2. 19 ; 5 ; 95
3. 54 ; 3 ; 162
4. 121 ; 4 ; 484
5. 1008
6. 5664

Page 19

	a	b	c	d	e	f
1.	69	690	86	860	204	2040
2.	148	1480	324	3240	657	6570
3.	1260	1500	2160	4340	5040	1600
4.	713	1386	540	595	864	
5.	1404	1517	448	2774	1288	

Page 20

1. 1440
2. 768
3. 3723
4. 3384
5. 4624
6. 6375
7. 1102
8. 2204

Page 21

	a	b	c	d	e
1.	546	736	2214	962	1102
2.	4176	972	2200	729	1638
3.	2002	6006	10291	9984	19505
4.	9855	5538	18590	12986	21924

Page 22

1. 7056	4. 8760	7. 40641
2. 5610	5. 23320	8. 39936
3. 3024	6. 57120	9. 26865

Page 23

	a	b	c	d
1.	632	63200	12843	1284300
2.	88608	109125	128928	110157
3.	86900	101913	901203	425088
4.	528525	668928	2323680	2261646

Page 24

1. 72504	4. 604800	7. 1636250
2. 74375	5. 329472	8. 2399375
3. 43680	6. 268544	

Page 27

	a	b	c	d	e	f
1.	3	3	2	4	2	2
2.	5	1	0	9	1	1
3.	7	7	6	6	4	7
4.	5	9	6	4	5	9
5.	3	9	8	8	5	9
6.	5	3	4	7	6	4
7.	8	8	8	8	4	6
8.	3	3	6	0	9	9
9.	5	7	5	6	7	6
10.	2	7	4	8	7	5

Page 28

1. 18 ; 6 ; 3	3. 6 ; 6 ; 1	5. 8
2. 18 ; 3 ; 6	4. 8	6. 6

Page 29

	a	b	c	d	e
1.	12	18	12	27	17
2.	37	29	15	112	256
3.	37	35	42	77	186

Page 30

1. 84 ; 6 ; 14	3. 24	5. 234
2. 91 ; 7 ; 13	4. 848 ; 4 ; 212	6. 58

Page 31

	a	b	c	d	e
1.	27 r1	17 r1	24 r1	25 r1	23 r1
2.	11 r6	13 r4	37 r2	31 r3	190
3.	57 r3	130 r3	137 r3	241 r1	138 r4

Page 32

1. 40	2. 53 ; 1	3. 148 ; 2

Page 33

	a	b	c
1.	276	220	2316
2.	126 r1	84 r1	190 r2
3.	352 r2	121	302 r3

Page 34

1. 48 ; 5	3. 325 ; 0	5. 247 ; 7
2. 29 ; 6	4. 191 ; 3	6. 2544 ; 1

Page 37

	a	b	c	d	e
1.	7	6	5	5 r4	7
2.	6 r2	5 r5	4 r10	6 r2	7 r8
3.	4	4	2 r20	4	3 r10

Page 38

1. 6	3. 4	5. 4 ; 4
2. 5 ; 3	4. 5 ; 7	6. 4

Page 39

	a	b	c	d	e
1.	27	16	19	35	67 r10
2.	12 r4	13 r10	12 r8	15	20 r4

Page 40

1. 32	3. 24 ; 6	5. 24 ; is not
2. 28 ; 2	4. 26	6. 52

Page 41

	a	b	c
1.	5 r8	6	4 r2
2.	6	21	26 r4
3.	13 r5	18 r24	18

Page 42

1. 4 ; 3	3. 7 ; 7	5. 35 ; 10
2. 6 ; 2	4. 28 ; 18	

Page 43

	a	b	c	d
1.	165	157	243	122
2.	213 r10	318 r17	167 r3	142 r62
3.	56	52	42 r10	52 r26

Page 44

1. 351	3. 84	5. 144
2. 342 ; 7	4. 72 ; 14	6. 212 ; 12

Page 45

	a	b	c	d
1.	27 r20	123 r10	5	4 r1
2.	217 r2	307	33	156
3.	6	9	10 r3	163 r8
4.	85	241	320	32
5.	400 r9	31	351	35 r24

Page 46

1. 576	2. 288	3. 144	4. 8064

Page 49

	a	b	c	d
1.	125	324 r6	85 r91	143
2.	3216	432 r10	1234	754

Page 50

1. 257	3. 245	5. 540
2. 75 ; 25	4. 316 ; 21	6. 600

Page 51

	a	b	c	d
1.	412	512	815	2146
2.	827 r22	3123 r30	2088 r16	705 r50

Page 52

1. 243	4. 203	7. 1218
2. 2452 ; 6	5. 406	
3. 543 ; 6	6. 812	

Page 53

	a	b
1.	2126 r10	612 r52
2.	726 r2	832 r5
3.	1268	1287 r12

Page 54

1. 438	3. 878 ; 33	5. 903 ; 7
2. 198	4. 872	6. 1806 ; 14

Page 55

	a	b	c	d
1.	1 r34	26 r3	145	1290 r17
2.	2 r6	22 r12	225	2250
3.	7 r3	8	35 r21	568
4.	1 r8	15 r9	80 r5	680 r5

Page 56

1. 57
2. is
3. 144 ; 6
4. 172 ; 54
5. 140
6. 14000

Page 59

	a	b
1.	7	70
2.	4	40
3.	2	20
4.	5	50

5. 65
6. 78
7. 32
8. 55

9-10. Have your teacher check your work.

Page 60

	a	b			a	b
1.	5	12		3.	91	86
2.	8	11				

Page 61

1.-3. Answers will vary.
4. taller
5. Answers will vary.
6. 1000
7. Sung-Chi ; 500

Page 62

	a	b
1.	50,000	6
2.	7	2
3.	90	8
4.	300	50

5. 3000 ; Ted ; 1000
6. Charles ; Su-Lyn
7. Answers will vary.

Page 63

	a	b	c
1.	10	3000	42
2.	1225	540	150

3. 54
4. 126
5. 140
6. 4375
7. 15,200

Page 64

1-2. Answers will vary.
3. 98 ; 588
4. 118 ; 840

Page 65

1. 10
2. Answers will vary.
3. 2
4. 5
5. 1

Page 66

	a	b
1.	7000	3
2.	2000	9
3.	20,000	48,000
4.	4	5

5. liter
6. Larry ; 500
7. 58
8. 1000

Page 67

1. 2
2. 2
3. 200
4. 2
5. 3
6. 17

Page 68

	a	b
1.	2000	6000
2.	9000	9000
3.	2	7
4.	3	8

5. penny ; 1000
6. 3
7. 1362
8. Judy ; 5

Page 71

	a	b			a	b
1.	72	38		4.	7	22
2.	72	227		5.	5	151
3.	15,840	5730		6.	5	30

7. 72 ; 70 ; Becky ; 2

Page 72

	a	b			a	b
1.	18	21		3.	12	19
2.	12	20		4.	12	26

Page 73

	a	b
1.	10	42
2.	64	4

3. 40
4. 96
5. 8094
6. 432
7. 270

Page 74

1. 68
2. 360 ; 8100
3. 500 ; 15,625
4. 16 ; 12
5. 11 ; 8 ; 38 ; 88

Page 75

	a	b			a	b
1.	4	22		4.	80	27
2.	2	98		5.	30	15
3.	32	7		6.	12	

7. 3 ; 5 ; Sallie ; 2

Page 76

1. 8 ; 4
2. 31 ; 62
3. 25 ; 50
4. 60
5. 15
6. 20
7. 10

Page 79

	a	b	c	d
1.	$\frac{1}{2};\frac{1}{2}$	$\frac{1}{3};\frac{2}{3}$	$\frac{1}{4};\frac{3}{4}$	$\frac{2}{3};\frac{1}{3}$
2.	$\frac{1}{8};\frac{7}{8}$	$\frac{3}{8};\frac{5}{8}$	$\frac{5}{8};\frac{3}{8}$	$\frac{7}{8};\frac{1}{8}$
3.	$\frac{2}{5};\frac{3}{5}$	$\frac{3}{5};\frac{2}{5}$	$\frac{4}{5};\frac{1}{5}$	$\frac{1}{5};\frac{4}{5}$
4.	$\frac{1}{3};\frac{2}{3}$	$\frac{2}{6};\frac{4}{6}$	$\frac{2}{3};\frac{1}{3}$	$\frac{4}{6};\frac{2}{6}$

Page 80

	a	b			a	b
1.	$\frac{3}{5}$	$\frac{2}{3}$		4.	$\frac{1}{5}$	$\frac{1}{6}$
2.	$\frac{4}{7}$	$\frac{4}{5}$		5.	$\frac{5}{9}$	$\frac{5}{9}$
3.	$\frac{5}{8}$	$\frac{3}{4}$				

6-7. Answers will vary.

Page 81

	a	b	c			a	b	c
1.	$\frac{2}{3}$	$\frac{1}{4}$	$\frac{4}{5}$		4.	$\frac{3}{5}$	$\frac{1}{8}$	$\frac{1}{2}$
2.	$\frac{3}{8}$	$\frac{4}{5}$	$\frac{3}{4}$		5.	$\frac{2}{3}$	$\frac{5}{6}$	$\frac{3}{4}$
3.	$\frac{7}{8}$	$\frac{3}{4}$	$\frac{5}{8}$					

Page 82

	a	b	c			a	b	c
1.	$\frac{1}{2}$	$\frac{1}{2}$	$\frac{1}{2}$		5.	$\frac{2}{5}$	$\frac{3}{7}$	$\frac{4}{5}$
2.	$\frac{1}{2}$	$\frac{1}{5}$	$\frac{1}{5}$		6.	$\frac{5}{6}$	$\frac{5}{9}$	$\frac{6}{7}$
3.	$\frac{1}{6}$	$\frac{2}{3}$	$\frac{2}{3}$		7.	$\frac{3}{5}$	$\frac{5}{6}$	$\frac{4}{5}$
4.	$\frac{2}{7}$	$\frac{2}{5}$	$\frac{1}{3}$		8.	$\frac{2}{3}$	$\frac{3}{7}$	$\frac{3}{4}$

Page 83

	a	b	c			a	b	c
1.	$2\frac{1}{4}$	$1\frac{1}{5}$	$1\frac{1}{8}$		4.	$2\frac{1}{7}$	$2\frac{2}{5}$	$2\frac{1}{9}$
2.	$2\frac{2}{3}$	$1\frac{4}{5}$	$2\frac{1}{3}$		5.	$3\frac{1}{7}$	$9\frac{1}{2}$	$5\frac{2}{5}$
3.	$1\frac{3}{4}$	$4\frac{5}{6}$	$4\frac{2}{3}$		6.	$4\frac{3}{8}$	$6\frac{1}{7}$	$9\frac{1}{6}$

Page 84

	a	b	c			a	b	c
1.	$\frac{7}{3}$	$\frac{7}{2}$	$\frac{19}{4}$		3.	$\frac{11}{5}$	$\frac{9}{7}$	$\frac{38}{7}$
2.	$\frac{34}{5}$	$\frac{27}{8}$	$\frac{23}{9}$		4.	$\frac{77}{12}$	$\frac{73}{10}$	$\frac{126}{15}$

Page 85

	a	b	c			a	b	c
1.	$3\frac{2}{3}$	$1\frac{1}{2}$	$2\frac{3}{4}$		3.	$2\frac{2}{5}$	$4\frac{1}{2}$	$3\frac{1}{3}$
2.	$4\frac{1}{4}$	$2\frac{3}{8}$	$1\frac{5}{6}$		4.	$2\frac{1}{5}$	$3\frac{1}{2}$	$6\frac{1}{3}$

Page 86

	a	b	c			a	b	c
1.	$\frac{3}{7}$	$\frac{4}{9}$	$\frac{3}{5}$		4.	$1\frac{1}{2}$	$2\frac{2}{3}$	$1\frac{2}{3}$
2.	$\frac{1}{3}$	$\frac{7}{8}$	$\frac{5}{7}$		5.	$1\frac{4}{5}$	$2\frac{1}{3}$	$3\frac{3}{5}$
3.	$1\frac{4}{5}$	$2\frac{2}{3}$	$1\frac{5}{7}$		6.	$4\frac{6}{7}$	$5\frac{2}{3}$	$2\frac{3}{4}$

Page 89

	a	b			a	b
1.	$\frac{1}{8}$	$\frac{1}{4}$		3.	$\frac{1}{10}$	$\frac{3}{10}$
2.	$\frac{1}{6}$	$\frac{1}{6}$				

Page 90

	a	b	c			a	b	c
1.		$\frac{2}{15}$	$\frac{5}{48}$		4.	$\frac{2}{35}$	$\frac{5}{12}$	$\frac{10}{21}$
2.	$\frac{3}{28}$	$\frac{5}{18}$	$\frac{12}{35}$		5.	$\frac{4}{15}$	$\frac{15}{32}$	$\frac{2}{15}$
3.	$\frac{8}{15}$	$\frac{7}{48}$	$\frac{2}{15}$					

Page 91

	a	b	c			a	b	c
1.	$\frac{5}{28}$	$\frac{3}{10}$	$\frac{21}{32}$		4.	$\frac{2}{9}$	$\frac{4}{15}$	$\frac{2}{7}$
2.	$\frac{6}{35}$	$\frac{7}{32}$	$\frac{4}{15}$		5.	$\frac{4}{7}$	$\frac{77}{96}$	$\frac{21}{80}$
3.	$\frac{3}{14}$	$\frac{3}{4}$	$\frac{1}{3}$					

Page 92

1.	$\frac{1}{2}$	3.	$\frac{1}{8}$	5.	$\frac{1}{3}$	7.	$\frac{3}{8}$
2.	$\frac{7}{10}$	4.	$\frac{1}{4}$	6.	$\frac{1}{3}$		

Page 93

	a	b	c		a	b	c
1.	$2\frac{1}{7}$	$7\frac{7}{8}$	$5\frac{5}{6}$	3.	6	$7\frac{1}{2}$	$3\frac{1}{5}$
2.	$3\frac{1}{3}$	$7\frac{7}{8}$	$9\frac{3}{5}$	4.	$10\frac{1}{2}$	6	$11\frac{2}{3}$

Page 94

1.	10	3.	8	5.	48	7.	$17\frac{1}{2}$
2.	20	4.	24	6.	$8\frac{3}{4}$		

Page 95

	a	b	c			a	b	c
1.	$22\frac{1}{2}$	$12\frac{1}{4}$	$6\frac{3}{8}$		3.	$19\frac{3}{5}$	$22\frac{2}{3}$	$32\frac{4}{7}$
2.	16	$11\frac{1}{4}$	$9\frac{1}{2}$		4.	$22\frac{2}{3}$	46	$23\frac{1}{3}$

Page 96

1.	$24\frac{1}{2}$	3.	$8\frac{3}{4}$	5.	$25\frac{1}{2}$	7.	15
2.	35	4.	$9\frac{3}{4}$	6.	30	8.	$53\frac{3}{4}$

Page 97

	a	b	c		a	b	c
1.	$5\frac{5}{24}$	$2\frac{11}{12}$	$3\frac{3}{20}$	3.	6	$7\frac{1}{2}$	12
2.	$11\frac{1}{5}$	$2\frac{6}{7}$	$1\frac{13}{15}$	4.	$5\frac{2}{5}$	$1\frac{27}{28}$	8

Page 98

1.	$7\frac{7}{8}$	3.	$11\frac{1}{4}$	5.	$18\frac{3}{4}$	7.	$65\frac{5}{8}$
2.	$6\frac{1}{8}$	4.	$110\frac{1}{4}$	6.	50		

Page 99

	a	b	c	d
1.	$\frac{3}{20}$	$\frac{6}{35}$	$\frac{2}{15}$	$\frac{35}{96}$
2.	$\frac{2}{7}$	$\frac{10}{21}$	$\frac{1}{12}$	$\frac{5}{16}$
3.	$2\frac{2}{5}$	$1\frac{1}{7}$	6	$2\frac{1}{4}$
4.	32	110	$23\frac{1}{3}$	$16\frac{2}{3}$
5.	10	$8\frac{2}{5}$	$11\frac{2}{3}$	2

Page 100

1.	$\frac{1}{2}$	3.	$\frac{3}{10}$	5.	81	7.	$9\frac{1}{3}$
2.	85	4.	$8\frac{3}{4}$	6.	$13\frac{1}{2}$		

Page 103

	a	b	c			a	b	c
1.	$\frac{2}{3}$	$\frac{3}{4}$	$\frac{5}{6}$		3.	$\frac{1}{6}$	$\frac{7}{9}$	$\frac{3}{5}$
2.	$\frac{5}{6}$	$\frac{4}{7}$	$\frac{7}{8}$		4.	$\frac{5}{8}$	$\frac{4}{5}$	$\frac{8}{9}$

Page 104

	a	b	c	d	e
1.	$\frac{2}{3}$	$\frac{6}{7}$	$\frac{7}{8}$	$\frac{3}{4}$	$\frac{4}{5}$
2.	$\frac{7}{9}$	$\frac{5}{8}$	$\frac{5}{6}$	$\frac{6}{7}$	$\frac{7}{10}$
3.	$\frac{3}{5}$	$\frac{5}{6}$	$\frac{3}{8}$	$\frac{4}{7}$	$\frac{4}{9}$
4.	$\frac{5}{9}$	$\frac{5}{7}$	$\frac{7}{8}$	$\frac{2}{5}$	$\frac{4}{7}$

Page 105

	a	b	c	d
1.	$1\frac{1}{3}$	$1\frac{2}{5}$	$\frac{1}{3}$	$\frac{1}{2}$
2.	$\frac{3}{4}$	$1\frac{1}{5}$	$1\frac{1}{2}$	$1\frac{1}{2}$
3.	1	$1\frac{4}{7}$	$1\frac{1}{2}$	1
4.	$1\frac{1}{5}$	1	$1\frac{4}{9}$	$1\frac{3}{5}$

Page 106

	a	b	c	d
1.	$3\frac{3}{5}$	$6\frac{1}{3}$	$5\frac{2}{5}$	$26\frac{1}{2}$
2.	$7\frac{1}{2}$	8	$4\frac{3}{5}$	$40\frac{2}{5}$
3.	7	$8\frac{2}{3}$	$13\frac{1}{2}$	$64\frac{1}{2}$
4.	$14\frac{1}{3}$	$14\frac{1}{5}$	18	$90\frac{1}{3}$

Page 107

	a	b	c			a	b	c
1.	8	6	10		3.	9	6	16
2.	5	4	9					

Answers Grade 5

Page 108

	a	b	c			a	b	c
1.	2	3	36		3.	2	10	12
2.	12	8	35		4.	2	4	36

Page 109

	a	b	c	d
1.	$\frac{9}{10}$	$\frac{11}{12}$	$\frac{11}{15}$	$\frac{7}{10}$
2.	$1\frac{13}{30}$	$\frac{13}{15}$	$\frac{19}{30}$	$1\frac{7}{24}$
3.	$1\frac{1}{12}$	$1\frac{7}{15}$	$1\frac{5}{12}$	$1\frac{5}{24}$

Page 110

	a	b	c	d
1.	$\frac{7}{8}$	$1\frac{1}{2}$	$\frac{4}{5}$	$1\frac{1}{12}$
2.	$\frac{11}{16}$	$\frac{2}{3}$	$\frac{7}{8}$	$1\frac{1}{2}$
3.	$1\frac{5}{16}$	$\frac{2}{3}$	$1\frac{1}{6}$	$1\frac{3}{8}$

Page 111

	a	b	c	d
1.	$\frac{5}{18}$	$\frac{5}{12}$	$\frac{23}{24}$	$\frac{11}{60}$
2.	$\frac{13}{24}$	$\frac{11}{12}$	$1\frac{11}{24}$	$\frac{27}{40}$
3.	$\frac{43}{60}$	$1\frac{5}{18}$	$\frac{11}{20}$	$1\frac{2}{15}$
4.	$1\frac{8}{15}$	$1\frac{19}{24}$	$1\frac{31}{40}$	$1\frac{1}{12}$

Page 112

1.	$1\frac{3}{8}$	3.	$1\frac{1}{4}$	5.	$\frac{7}{8}$	7.	$1\frac{1}{20}$
2.	$\frac{7}{12}$	4.	$1\frac{5}{12}$	6.	$1\frac{9}{16}$		

Page 113

	a	b	c	d
1.	$8\frac{11}{24}$	$7\frac{1}{2}$	$10\frac{1}{12}$	$3\frac{1}{4}$
2.	$6\frac{1}{6}$	$8\frac{1}{4}$	$4\frac{5}{12}$	$4\frac{1}{10}$
3.	$10\frac{5}{8}$	$5\frac{11}{15}$	$6\frac{7}{10}$	$7\frac{7}{8}$
4.	7	$3\frac{7}{8}$	$16\frac{1}{4}$	$14\frac{1}{2}$

Page 114

1.	$4\frac{1}{4}$	3.	$4\frac{9}{10}$
2.	17	4.	$6\frac{1}{3}$

Page 115

	a	b	c	d
1.	$\frac{1}{4}$	$9\frac{11}{24}$	$7\frac{1}{12}$	$1\frac{5}{16}$
2.	$7\frac{17}{20}$	$1\frac{33}{70}$	$4\frac{13}{20}$	$1\frac{1}{6}$
3.	$1\frac{3}{14}$	$6\frac{14}{15}$	$6\frac{1}{6}$	$\frac{13}{14}$
4.	$3\frac{4}{15}$	$\frac{23}{36}$	$1\frac{1}{3}$	$11\frac{5}{9}$
5.	$\frac{7}{10}$	$1\frac{17}{18}$	$9\frac{1}{10}$	$17\frac{7}{12}$

Page 116

1.	82	3.	$11\frac{5}{8}$	5.	$5\frac{7}{12}$
2.	$4\frac{1}{4}$	4.	$101\frac{1}{10}$	6.	$3\frac{1}{8}$

Page 117

	a	b	c	d
1.	$\frac{5}{9}$	$\frac{5}{7}$	$1\frac{4}{9}$	$1\frac{1}{8}$
2.	$\frac{13}{15}$	$1\frac{3}{20}$	$1\frac{1}{4}$	$\frac{11}{12}$
3.	$1\frac{17}{24}$	$\frac{3}{4}$	$\frac{9}{10}$	$1\frac{7}{24}$
4.	$\frac{3}{5}$	$2\frac{4}{9}$	$8\frac{7}{24}$	$6\frac{1}{12}$

Page 117 (continued)

5.	$\frac{8}{15}$	$\frac{19}{20}$	$3\frac{1}{2}$	$6\frac{3}{4}$

Page 118

1.	$1\frac{1}{4}$	3.	$1\frac{1}{4}$	5.	$6\frac{1}{4}$	7.	$51\frac{3}{8}$
2.	$1\frac{7}{30}$	4.	$1\frac{3}{5}$	6.	6		

Page 121

	a	b	c	d	e
1.	$\frac{1}{9}$	$\frac{2}{5}$	$\frac{4}{9}$	$\frac{1}{2}$	$\frac{2}{3}$
2.	$\frac{2}{7}$	$\frac{1}{4}$	$\frac{3}{5}$	$\frac{1}{5}$	$\frac{4}{9}$
3.	$\frac{3}{7}$	$\frac{7}{9}$	$\frac{1}{2}$	$\frac{1}{6}$	$\frac{1}{5}$
4.	$\frac{2}{5}$	$\frac{1}{3}$	$\frac{2}{5}$	$\frac{1}{3}$	$\frac{3}{4}$

Page 122

	a	b	c	d
1.	$1\frac{3}{4}$	$2\frac{1}{3}$	$5\frac{4}{5}$	$4\frac{2}{3}$
2.	$3\frac{1}{4}$	$4\frac{3}{5}$	$3\frac{3}{5}$	$5\frac{1}{6}$
3.	$\frac{1}{2}$	$1\frac{1}{8}$	$\frac{7}{8}$	$1\frac{7}{10}$

Page 123

	a	b	c	d
1.	$3\frac{2}{9}$	$2\frac{5}{7}$	$5\frac{1}{2}$	$4\frac{1}{4}$
2.	$3\frac{2}{3}$	$5\frac{3}{5}$	$5\frac{3}{4}$	$3\frac{4}{9}$
3.	$2\frac{1}{3}$	$2\frac{1}{2}$	$1\frac{3}{5}$	1

Page 124

1.	$5\frac{1}{2}$	3.	$1\frac{1}{4}$	5.	$\frac{1}{2}$
2.	$2\frac{1}{3}$	4.	$\frac{1}{2}$	6.	$3\frac{2}{3}$

Page 125

	a	b	c	d
1.	$\frac{4}{15}$	$\frac{13}{20}$	$\frac{3}{8}$	$\frac{2}{9}$
2.	$\frac{1}{2}$	$\frac{1}{2}$	$\frac{1}{3}$	$\frac{1}{2}$
3.	$\frac{2}{5}$	$\frac{17}{42}$	$\frac{11}{20}$	$\frac{3}{4}$

Page 126

1.	$\frac{1}{3}$	3.	$\frac{19}{30}$	5.	$\frac{5}{16}$	7.	$\frac{19}{36}$
2.	$\frac{1}{6}$	4.	$\frac{1}{6}$	6.	$\frac{1}{6}$		

Page 127

	a	b	c	d
1.	$\frac{11}{24}$	$\frac{7}{12}$	$\frac{23}{40}$	$\frac{11}{18}$
2.	$\frac{3}{10}$	$\frac{17}{24}$	$\frac{7}{15}$	$\frac{1}{18}$
3.	$\frac{1}{3}$	$\frac{1}{3}$	$\frac{13}{24}$	$\frac{1}{20}$
4.	$\frac{2}{9}$	$\frac{13}{24}$	$\frac{1}{6}$	$\frac{1}{12}$

Page 128

1.	Cal ; $\frac{2}{5}$	3.	$\frac{9}{20}$	5.	Cal ; $\frac{7}{20}$
2.	Cal ; $\frac{1}{5}$	4.	$\frac{1}{10}$		

Page 129

	a	b	c	d
1.	$1\frac{7}{12}$	$2\frac{9}{10}$	$4\frac{19}{24}$	$3\frac{1}{9}$
2.	$2\frac{1}{24}$	$1\frac{3}{4}$	$1\frac{1}{14}$	$4\frac{3}{10}$
3.	$4\frac{11}{40}$	$2\frac{7}{9}$	$1\frac{1}{6}$	$\frac{19}{40}$
4.	$3\frac{5}{9}$	$1\frac{13}{35}$	$1\frac{41}{60}$	$1\frac{17}{24}$

Page 130

1. $\frac{3}{4}$ 3. $2\frac{4}{5}$ 5. $1\frac{1}{2}$

2. $\frac{5}{6}$ 4. $\frac{7}{12}$ 6. $2\frac{9}{16}$

Page 131

	a	b	c	d
1.	$\frac{1}{3}$	$\frac{3}{8}$	$\frac{11}{16}$	$\frac{3}{4}$
2.	$\frac{2}{15}$	$\frac{1}{10}$	$\frac{1}{2}$	$\frac{1}{6}$
3.	$\frac{1}{6}$	$\frac{7}{40}$	$\frac{1}{4}$	$\frac{1}{2}$
4.	$3\frac{3}{10}$	$2\frac{1}{3}$	$2\frac{2}{5}$	$1\frac{3}{4}$
5.	$\frac{19}{20}$	$2\frac{3}{7}$	$\frac{1}{2}$	$1\frac{9}{10}$

Page 132

1. $8\frac{1}{2}$ 3. $\frac{2}{15}$ 5. $1\frac{3}{4}$ 7. $4\frac{3}{8}$

2. $1\frac{3}{4}$ 4. $1\frac{3}{4}$ 6. $1\frac{5}{6}$

Page 133

	a	b	c	d
1.	$\frac{5}{9}$	$\frac{4}{7}$	$\frac{1}{4}$	$\frac{3}{5}$
2.	$1\frac{2}{3}$	$1\frac{1}{3}$	$3\frac{1}{2}$	$\frac{4}{5}$
3.	$\frac{1}{12}$	$\frac{2}{15}$	$\frac{1}{4}$	$\frac{2}{9}$
4.	$\frac{1}{8}$	$\frac{1}{3}$	$\frac{7}{12}$	$\frac{37}{60}$
5.	$1\frac{17}{24}$	$2\frac{9}{10}$	$1\frac{43}{60}$	$5\frac{11}{36}$

Page 134

1. $1\frac{5}{6}$ 3. $\frac{11}{12}$

2. $2\frac{3}{4}$ 4. $7\frac{1}{6}$

Page 137

1. line AB   4. line MN   7. line ZX
2. line segment 5. line segment 8. line EP
   FG   RS   9. line segment
3. line segment 6. line segment   VT
   CE   KI   10. $\overset{\bullet\qquad\bullet}{H\qquad Q}$

Page 138

	a	b	c
1.	$\angle$ XYZ or $\angle$ ZYX ; 60°	$\angle$ FCD or $\angle$ DCF ; 90°	$\angle$ GMS or $\angle$ SMG ; 20°
2.	$\angle$ SBD or $\angle$ DBS ; 130°	$\angle$ VWK or $\angle$ KWV ; 65°	$\angle$ NPQ or $\angle$ QPN ; 93°

Page 139

1. b. ; h.   4. d. ; i.   7. i.   10. square
2. a.   5. f.   8. a.   11. c. ; e.
3. c.   6. e. ; g.   9. h.

Page 140

1. Have your teacher check your work.
   FH or HF; FI or IF; JG or GJ; JH or HJ; IG or GI
2. No   6. Yes
3. QP, PQ, PR, RP, SP,   7. Have your teacher
   or PS   check your work.
4. SR or RS   8. 9
5. Have your teacher   9. Yes
   check your work.

Page 141

1. squares (or   4. edge   7. Yes
   rectangles)   5. vertex   8. Yes
2. rectangles   6. face   9. Yes
3. triangle

Page vii

	a	b	c	d	e	f	g	h
1.	4	8	2	12	8	4	9	5
2.	9	5	10	8	12	10	13	12
3.	11	0	11	11	14	8	9	11
4.	6	4	7	2	13	9	10	11
5.	9	13	12	5	10	3	7	5
6.	15	7	11	8	6	10	17	9
7.	6	11	14	18	13	10	12	10
8.	14	7	7	11	7	13	17	9
9.	16	8	10	14	15	12	12	16
10.	15	16	6	13	8	15	9	14

Page viii

	a	b	c	d	e	f	g	h
1.	7	4	12	5	4	5	11	6
2.	6	8	3	13	16	8	6	9
3.	7	8	11	15	18	3	13	13
4.	12	12	10	12	8	4	14	2
5.	17	6	0	6	14	13	11	11
6.	7	16	11	10	8	10	12	9
7.	7	9	11	14	10	14	9	11
8.	15	10	15	8	9	17	10	9
9.	12	8	7	11	15	5	9	14
10.	9	16	8	13	12	10	13	10

Page ix

	a	b	c	d	e	f	g	h
1.	1	8	5	3	5	3	1	5
2.	2	7	2	9	0	7	3	4
3.	0	2	7	6	4	6	2	7
4.	9	9	4	3	0	4	5	8
5.	9	9	1	4	6	7	3	4
6.	3	8	1	9	4	5	1	8
7.	0	7	2	7	0	8	2	1
8.	4	9	8	8	8	6	7	5
9.	8	5	7	5	9	2	3	7
10.	9	6	0	6	8	6	6	9

Page x

	a	b	c	d	e	f	g	h
1.	4	8	8	6	9	5	9	4
2.	4	4	7	1	7	1	9	0
3.	6	2	8	0	4	6	5	6
4.	9	2	8	3	6	7	6	4
5.	5	9	7	0	7	7	9	2
6.	7	7	5	4	5	1	9	6
7.	3	5	3	8	8	1	6	4
8.	3	2	7	4	8	5	8	5
9.	8	5	0	4	6	5	6	3
10.	8	9	7	1	9	2	9	0

Page xi

	a	b	c	d	e	f	g	h
1.	9	8	21	4	27	45	64	12
2.	36	49	0	30	18	2	42	24
3.	12	0	36	35	32	56	15	0
4.	0	72	24	0	8	56	28	48
5.	10	20	28	0	36	4	81	1
6.	8	5	42	63	3	40	15	18
7.	12	6	25	48	24	72	0	7
8.	54	0	32	9	0	16	63	27
9.	30	45	9	10	35	18	20	14
10.	6	12	24	16	0	21	40	54

Page xii

	a	b	c	d	e	f	g	h
1.	25	12	1	21	12	0	8	12
2.	18	63	2	9	16	4	45	16
3.	18	0	30	3	10	4	0	27
4.	15	16	24	14	0	36	64	0
5.	18	24	0	36	30	24	6	0
6.	5	28	32	8	54	35	63	56
7.	9	7	35	0	20	81	40	32
8.	48	40	45	36	49	0	15	27
9.	10	18	72	6	48	28	56	54
10.	20	42	72	24	0	42	21	14

Page xiii

	a	b	c	d	e	f	g
1.	3	2	5	3	3	3	9
2.	7	2	0	7	9	3	2
3.	4	4	4	6	4	1	4
4.	0	1	5	8	2	3	9
5.	1	0	8	7	5	3	2
6.	9	9	0	4	8	0	7
7.	6	7	8	6	9	5	6
8.	0	7	8	3	1	2	0
9.	4	5	5	7	1	7	8
10.	5	1	0	6	8	2	1
11.	8	4	6	8	7	6	9
12.	6	9	5	2	3	9	5

Page xiv

	a	b	c	d	e	f	g
1.	6	7	1	9	0	9	9
2.	9	2	8	8	2	7	9
3.	0	3	8	3	6	9	0
4.	6	7	8	7	4	2	1
5.	5	0	5	2	2	2	5
6.	5	4	6	3	1	8	0
7.	6	5	0	7	3	3	6
8.	6	5	5	8	2	2	7
9.	4	0	7	3	5	8	0
10.	4	9	1	3	3	2	6
11.	1	4	5	4	4	8	9
12.	4	3	9	4	0	7	6

	a	b	c	d	e
1.	68	85	118	124	87
2.	61	49	81	78	69
3.	778	981	405	1304	1243
4.	533	158	351	1087	918
5.	8031	11257	55990	90613	61007
6.	3812	1876	49112	3769	13949
7.	137	147	1002	17069	168398
8.	165	1684	1795	24001	226421

Page 2

1. 33 ; 24 ; 57
2. Kennedy ; 9
3. 43 ; 36 ; Kennedy ; 7

Page 13

	a	b	c	d	e
1.	78	691	5402	11130	125008
2.	53	182	1457	9048	7738
3.	71	1569	1059	13089	155316
4.	6365	5655	8886	89065	65559
5.	2320 ; 907 ; 3227			7. 789	
6.	6418				

Page 14

	a	b	c	d
1.	48	70	924	6102
2.	713	1476	2295	3393
3.	3146	13946	15686	25488
4.	39483	268272	72501	86205
5.	1319172	584640	2224288	2664025

Page 25

	a	b	c	d
1.	93	75	1656	4081
2.	299	1092	646	2385
3.	3813	29750	14075	71145
4.	28116	159138	27648	316030
5.	380952	251888	1041390	2529792

Page 26

	a	b	c	d
1.	9	9	15	23
2.	34	74	157	480
3.	513	918	1015	1721
4.	21 r3	37 r1	28 r2	260 r1
5.	23 r5	2306 r2	717 r1	1226 r4

Page 35

	a	b	c	d
1.	24	12	26 r1	13 r3
2.	183	35	87 r6	323 r1
3.	215	1304	382 r2	2107 r2
4.	28	12 r4	11 r6	39
5.	314	2114 r1	368 r2	1201

Page 36

	a	b	c	d
1.	6	7	5 r5	6 r5
2.	13	26	48 r10	23 r21
3.	132	98	56 r10	112 r22
4.	48	52 r20	17 r4	4
5.	126	40	37 r2	38

Page 47

	a	b	c	d
1.	6	6 r11	8 r6	4
2.	15 r10	78	31	42 r2

Page 47 (continued)

	a	b	c	d
3.	121 r10	45	53 r65	156
4.	13	122 r3	4 r11	4
5.	27	83 r20	20 r13	2 r15

Page 48

	a	b	c	d
1.	3	30	300	3000
2.	1120	2372 r15	2222	858
3.	2131 r21	6123 r10	2517 r15	2117 r7
4.	452	576	317 r10	444

Page 57

	a	b	c	d
1.	9	17	41	105
2.	268	123	112	127 r52
3.	742	340 r37	421 r12	735
4.	935	2005 r11	1770 r20	1199 r1
5.	1001	401	3000 r6	801

Page 58

	a	b		a	b
1.	6	60	7.	8000	16,000
2.	4	38	8.	5000	5000
3.	10	6	9.	2000	140
4.	60	225	10.	40,000	4200
5.	70	2800	11.	3000	35,000
6.	900	49,000	12.	60,000	34,000

Page 69

	a	b		a	b
1.	5	50	6.	7	30
2.	7	70	7.	6000	300
3.	20	24	8.	4000	3
4.	80	375	9.	2000	8000
5.	50	2	10.	7000	5

Page 70

	a	b		a	b
1.	48	54	5.	3	7
2.	8	8	6.	2	18
3.	15	46	7.	2	102
4.	5280	100			

	a	b	c
8.	18	24	16
9.	20	14	25

Page 77

	a	b		a	b
1.	14	108	5.	15	27
2.	9	12	6.	118	22
3.	3	360	7.	71	14
4.	22	11			

	a	b	c
8.	28	13	18
9.	27	64	12

Page 78

	a	b	c	d
1.	$\frac{1}{4}$	$\frac{1}{2}$	$\frac{7}{8}$	$\frac{2}{5}$
2.	$\frac{2}{3}$	$\frac{1}{2}$	$\frac{3}{4}$	
3.	$1\frac{1}{6}$	$2\frac{2}{3}$	$3\frac{2}{5}$	
4.	$\frac{13}{4}$	$\frac{13}{2}$	$\frac{23}{6}$	
5.	$1\frac{3}{4}$	$3\frac{1}{3}$	$6\frac{1}{2}$	

Page 87

	a	b	c	d
1.	$\frac{1}{2}$	$\frac{1}{2}$	$\frac{2}{3}$	$\frac{1}{2}$
2.	$\frac{2}{3}$	$\frac{3}{4}$	$\frac{2}{3}$	$\frac{3}{4}$
3.	$2\frac{1}{2}$	$1\frac{2}{3}$	$2\frac{1}{4}$	$5\frac{1}{3}$
4.	$\frac{3}{2}$	$\frac{15}{8}$	$\frac{14}{3}$	$\frac{35}{6}$
5.	$1\frac{4}{5}$	$2\frac{1}{4}$	$3\frac{1}{3}$	$6\frac{1}{2}$

Page 88

	a	b	c			a	b	c
1.	$\frac{6}{35}$	$\frac{21}{32}$	$\frac{16}{25}$	4.		$12\frac{4}{5}$	18	11
2.	$\frac{7}{12}$	$\frac{1}{3}$	$\frac{3}{8}$	5.		$5\frac{5}{6}$	$2\frac{7}{10}$	$3\frac{3}{4}$
3.	$2\frac{2}{3}$	$2\frac{1}{2}$	$6\frac{1}{4}$					

Page 101

	a	b	c			a	b	c
1.	$\frac{35}{48}$	$\frac{12}{35}$	$\frac{2}{15}$	4.		$9\frac{3}{5}$	$25\frac{1}{2}$	$3\frac{2}{3}$
2.	$\frac{5}{9}$	$\frac{1}{3}$	$\frac{3}{8}$	5.		$1\frac{1}{5}$	6	$2\frac{1}{2}$
3.	$4\frac{4}{5}$	$7\frac{1}{2}$	15	6.		$2\frac{2}{15}$	$8\frac{1}{3}$	$2\frac{7}{16}$

Page 102

	a	b	c	d
1.	$\frac{1}{3}$	$\frac{1}{2}$	$\frac{7}{9}$	1
2.	$1\frac{1}{6}$	$1\frac{3}{8}$	$1\frac{1}{10}$	$\frac{17}{20}$
3.	$10\frac{3}{4}$	$7\frac{9}{10}$	$6\frac{1}{12}$	$6\frac{5}{6}$
4.	$5\frac{19}{24}$	$5\frac{19}{20}$	$1\frac{5}{12}$	$6\frac{5}{6}$
5.	$1\frac{5}{12}$	$9\frac{5}{8}$	$5\frac{1}{10}$	$10\frac{1}{2}$

Page 119

	a	b	c	d
1.	$\frac{2}{5}$	1	$1\frac{1}{2}$	$\frac{5}{7}$
2.	$\frac{7}{8}$	$1\frac{1}{20}$	$1\frac{3}{10}$	$1\frac{7}{12}$
3.	$6\frac{19}{30}$	$6\frac{8}{9}$	$3\frac{11}{12}$	$6\frac{3}{4}$
4.	$6\frac{9}{20}$	$6\frac{2}{15}$	$9\frac{11}{16}$	$16\frac{1}{2}$
5.	$7\frac{9}{20}$	$10\frac{29}{60}$	$48\frac{1}{2}$	$76\frac{3}{10}$

Page 120

	a	b	c	d
1.	$\frac{1}{2}$	$\frac{2}{3}$	$\frac{2}{3}$	$\frac{2}{3}$
2.	$3\frac{3}{5}$	$1\frac{1}{3}$	$4\frac{5}{7}$	$2\frac{1}{2}$
3.	$\frac{1}{6}$	$\frac{1}{6}$	$\frac{5}{9}$	$\frac{1}{8}$
4.	$\frac{1}{2}$	$\frac{23}{40}$	$\frac{1}{2}$	$\frac{1}{4}$
5.	$2\frac{1}{2}$	$2\frac{5}{24}$	$\frac{3}{10}$	$1\frac{8}{15}$

Page 135

	a	b	c	d
1.	$\frac{1}{5}$	$\frac{2}{15}$	$\frac{1}{8}$	$\frac{2}{3}$
2.	$\frac{1}{3}$	$\frac{1}{8}$	$\frac{2}{3}$	$\frac{1}{12}$
3.	$\frac{3}{8}$	$\frac{13}{18}$	$\frac{5}{8}$	$\frac{1}{6}$
4.	$3\frac{1}{2}$	$2\frac{1}{10}$	$5\frac{1}{6}$	$1\frac{1}{2}$
5.	$2\frac{1}{12}$	$2\frac{7}{8}$	$1\frac{1}{3}$	$\frac{9}{10}$

Page 136

1. line MN
2. line segment PR
3. ∠CAB or ∠BAC
4. ∠TVX or ∠XVT
5. ∠YDQ or ∠QDY
6. g.
7. b.
8. d.
9. a.

Page 142

1. line segment SR
2. line XY
3. ∠BCD or ∠DCB; 70°
4. ∠MNL or ∠LNM; 90°
5. ∠TUV or ∠VUT; 165°
6. c.
7. f.
8. d.
9. d.
10. c.

Page 143

	a	b	c	d
1.	93	170	1073	165504
2.	57	179	654	1272
3.	390	1323	6800	37800
4.	1036	3680	18600	213384
5.	16	123	355 r3	100 r38

Page 144

	a	b	c	d
6.	18 r2	62	34 r16	197 r6
7.	7	20 r6	33 r61	1316 r43

	a	b			a	b
8.	1800	3	11.		24	130
9.	21000	300000	12.		18 ; 18	260 ; 3600
10.	1	1960				

Page 145

	a	b	c	d	e
1.	93	162	933	128580	24207
2.	45	113	288	22151	66859
3.	438	992	3925	3870	13440
4.	972	2360	58473	81004	2079848

	a	b	c	d
5.	13	116	414 r3	121 r11
6.	19 r2	57 r3	20 r35	297 r37

Page 146

	a	b	c	d
7.	7 r2	117 r2	26 r15	4590 r1
8.	3 r15	21	99 r17	409 r2

	a	b			a	b
9.	1600	6000	13.		72	5
10.	17000	9	14.		12	102
11.	9000	30000	15.		26 ; 40	12 ; 8
12.	3	5305				

Page 147

	a	b	c			a	b	c
16.	$\frac{1}{3}$	$\frac{4}{5}$	$4\frac{3}{8}$	19.		$\frac{8}{15}$	$1\frac{7}{8}$	9
17.	$6\frac{2}{3}$	$3\frac{1}{3}$	$10\frac{1}{3}$	20.		$2\frac{1}{2}$	10	$8\frac{1}{3}$
18.	$\frac{2}{15}$	$\frac{7}{24}$	$\frac{6}{35}$	21.		$3\frac{1}{2}$	62	10

	a	b	c	d
22.	$\frac{4}{5}$	$\frac{5}{7}$	$\frac{3}{4}$	$\frac{3}{5}$
23.	$3\frac{1}{2}$	$21\frac{1}{3}$	$1\frac{1}{10}$	$1\frac{1}{8}$
24.	$1\frac{1}{6}$	$1\frac{17}{30}$	$9\frac{1}{2}$	$22\frac{5}{12}$

Page 148

	a	b	c	d
25.	$\frac{2}{5}$	$6\frac{2}{5}$	$4\frac{1}{2}$	$4\frac{1}{4}$
26.	$\frac{5}{8}$	$\frac{11}{18}$	$1\frac{5}{24}$	$5\frac{1}{40}$
27.	$\frac{1}{6}$	$\frac{7}{30}$	$1\frac{11}{24}$	$2\frac{17}{20}$

28. line AB or line BA
29. ∠DEF or ∠FED
30. circle
31. pentagon
32. quadrilateral
33. triangle

SPECTRUM

All our workbooks meet school curriculum guidelines and correspond to
The McGraw-Hill Companies classroom textbooks.

DOLCH Sight Word Activities

The DOLCH Sight Word Activities workbooks use the classic Dolch list of 220 basic vocabulary words that make up from 50% to 75% of all reading matter that children ordinarily encounter. Since these words are ordinarily recognized on sight, they are called *sight words*. Volume 1 includes 110 sight words. Volume 2 covers the remainder of the list. 160 pages. Answer key included.

TITLE	ISBN	PRICE
Grades K-1 Vol. 1	1-56189-917-8	$9.95
Grades K-1 Vol. 2	1-56189-918-6	$9.95

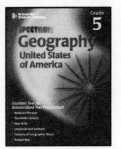

GEOGRAPHY

Full-color, three-part lessons strengthen geography knowledge and map reading skills. Focusing on five geographic themes including location, place, human/environmental interaction, movement, and regions. Over 150 pages. Glossary of geographical terms and answer key included.

TITLE	ISBN	PRICE
Grade 3, Communities	1-56189-963-1	$8.95
Grade 4, Regions	1-56189-964-X	$8.95
Grade 5, USA	1-56189-965-8	$8.95
Grade 6, World	1-56189-966-6	$8.95

MATH

Features easy-to-follow instructions that give students a clear path to success. This series has comprehensive coverage of the basic skills, helping children to master math fundamentals. Over 150 pages. Answer key included.

TITLE	ISBN	PRICE
Grade K	1-56189-900-3	$8.95
Grade 1	1-56189-901-1	$8.95
Grade 2	1-56189-902-X	$8.95
Grade 3	1-56189-903-8	$8.95
Grade 4	1-56189-904-6	$8.95
Grade 5	1-56189-905-4	$8.95
Grade 6	1-56189-906-2	$8.95
Grade 7	1-56189-907-0	$8.95
Grade 8	1-56189-908-9	$8.95

PHONICS/WORD STUDY

Provides everything children need to build multiple skills in language. Focusing on phonics, structural analysis, and dictionary skills, this series also offers creative ideas for using phonics and word study skills in other language areas. Over 200 pages. Answer key included.

TITLE	ISBN	PRICE
Grade K	1-56189-940-2	$8.95
Grade 1	1-56189-941-0	$8.95
Grade 2	1-56189-942-9	$8.95
Grade 3	1-56189-943-7	$8.95
Grade 4	1-56189-944-5	$8.95
Grade 5	1-56189-945-3	$8.95
Grade 6	1-56189-946-1	$8.95

ENRICHMENT MATH AND READING

Books in this series offer advanced math and reading for students excelling in grades 3–6. Lessons follow the same curriculum children are being taught in school while presenting the material in a way that children feel challenged. 160 pages. Answer key included.

TITLE	ISBN	PRICE
Grade 3	1-57768-503-2	$8.95
Grade 4	1-57768-504-0	$8.95
Grade 5	1-57768-505-9	$8.95
Grade 6	1-57768-506-7	$8.95

Prices subject to change without notice.

READING

This full-color series creates an enjoyable reading environment, even for below-average readers. Each book contains captivating content, colorful characters, and compelling illustrations, so children are eager to find out what happens next. Over 150 pages. Answer key included.

TITLE	ISBN	PRICE
Grade K	1-56189-910-0	$8.95
Grade 1	1-56189-911-9	$8.95
Grade 2	1-56189-912-7	$8.95
Grade 3	1-56189-913-5	$8.95
Grade 4	1-56189-914-3	$8.95
Grade 5	1-56189-915-1	$8.95
Grade 6	1-56189-916-X	$8.95

SPELLING

This full-color series links spelling to reading and writing, and increases skills in words and meanings, consonant and vowel spellings, and proofreading practice. Over 200 pages. Speller dictionary and answer key included.

TITLE	ISBN	PRICE
Grade 1	1-56189-921-6	$8.95
Grade 2	1-56189-922-4	$8.95
Grade 3	1-56189-923-2	$8.95
Grade 4	1-56189-924-0	$8.95
Grade 5	1-56189-925-9	$8.95
Grade 6	1-56189-926-7	$8.95

WRITING

Lessons focus on creative and expository writing using clearly stated objectives and pre-writing exercises. Eight essential reading skills are applied. Activities include main idea, sequence, comparison, detail, fact and opinion, cause and effect, making a point, and point of view. Over 130 pages. Answer key included.

TITLE	ISBN	PRICE
Grade 1	1-56189-931-3	$8.95
Grade 2	1-56189-932-1	$8.95
Grade 3	1-56189-933-X	$8.95
Grade 4	1-56189-934-8	$8.95
Grade 5	1-56189-935-6	$8.95
Grade 6	1-56189-936-4	$8.95
Grade 7	1-56189-937-2	$8.95
Grade 8	1-56189-938-0	$8.95

TEST PREP

Prepares children to do their best on current editions of the five major standardized tests. Activities reinforce test-taking skills through examples, tips, practice, and timed exercises. Subjects include reading, math, language arts, writing, social studies, and science. Over 150 pages. Answer key included.

TITLE	ISBN	PRICE
Grades 1-2	1-57768-672-1	$9.95
Grade 3	1-57768-673-X	$9.95
Grade 4	1-57768-674-8	$9.95
Grade 5	1-57768-675-6	$9.95
Grade 6	1-57768-676-4	$9.95
Grade 7	1-57768-677-2	$9.95
Grade 8	1-57768-678-0	$9.95

LANGUAGE ARTS

Encourages creativity and builds confidence by making writing fun! Seventy-two four-part lessons strengthen writing skills by focusing on parts of speech, word usage, sentence structure, punctuation, and proofreading. Each level includes a Writer's Handbook at the end of the book that offers writing tips. This series is based on the highly respected SRA/McGraw-Hill language arts series. More than 180 full-color pages. Answer key included.

TITLE	ISBN	PRICE
Grade 2	1-56189-952-6	$8.95
Grade 3	1-56189-953-4	$8.95
Grade 4	1-56189-954-2	$8.95
Grade 5	1-56189-955-0	$8.95
Grade 6	1-56189-956-9	$8.95

Prices subject to change without notice.

PRESCHOOL

Learning Letters offers comprehensive instruction and practice in following directions, recognizing and writing upper- and lowercase letters, and beginning phonics. Math Readiness features activities that teach such important skills as counting, identifying numbers, creating patterns, and recognizing "same and different." Basic Concepts and Skills offers exercises that help preschoolers identify colors, read and write words, identify simple shapes, and more. 160 pages.

TITLE	ISBN	PRICE
Learning Letters	1-57768-329-3	$8.95
Math Readiness	1-57768-339-0	$8.95
Basic Concepts and Skills	1-57768-349-8	$8.95